Victory Over Debt

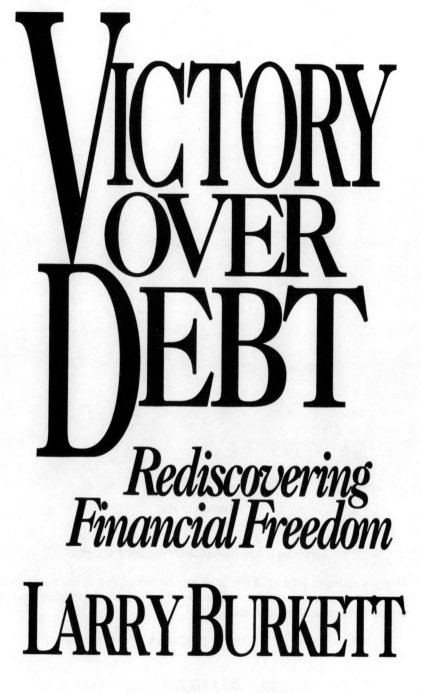

VICTORY OVER DEBT

Rediscovering Financial Freedom

LARRY BURKETT

NORTHFIELD PUBLISHING
CHICAGO

© 1992 by
NORTHFIELD PUBLISHING
A DIVISION OF MBI
CHICAGO, IL

This book is a revision of *Debt-Free Living* © 1989.

ISBN: 1-881273-00-8

3 5 7 9 10 8 6 4

Printed in the United States of America

Contents

PART THREE: Overview of Credit, Debt, and Borrowing

Introduction

Of all the problems facing families and individuals in the late twentieth century, none is more distressing than that of debt. Let me differentiate between debt and what is normally termed credit.

Credit, in and of itself, is not necessarily bad. It is merely a temporary extension of one's income-earning ability.

Debt, however, is the overextension of that ability. Literally, it is an unrealistic presumption upon future earnings. When you buy things on credit that you cannot afford to own, you do not avoid the consequences; you simply delay them, and often make them much worse.

Too often credit is used to delay making critical decisions until it is too late. This certainly can be witnessed when young couples buy homes and even making the monthly payments is dependent upon "ideal" circumstances—two incomes with uninterrupted earnings. Thus even normal events such as a pregnancy or illness often plunge them into unmanageable debt.

There is a predictable cycle that takes place whenever a couple, and to a lesser degree a single person, get into debt. The first phase is denial. The problem is ignored in the hope that it will somehow magically cure itself. Too often, a husband pushes the financial problems off on his wife and expects her to "stretch" the money to fit the debt (or vice versa if the wife is handling the money).

The next phase for the sensitive one in the marriage is fear and frustration when the creditors begin to harass through nasty letters or telephone calls. This will normally stir up enough stress to motivate even the most nonchalant spouse to proceed to the next step: a bill-consolidation loan. Thus a home equity or a family loan is used to consolidate most of the accumulated bills into one loan that requires a smaller monthly payment. As a result, the financial pressures are relieved somewhat. Unfortunately though, most people who use consolidation loans find themselves in even greater debt within a few months because they have returned to using the paid-off credit cards and now have those payments in addition to paying off the consolidation loan.

The next phase (at least for married couples) usually starts with the husband saying, "I can't stand all this pressure. I think we need a new car." And, in fact, most people in financial stress will buy something new because, in our society, the ability to buy new things is often equated with self-worth. Obviously this only compounds the problems. By the fifth year of marriage, nearly one half of all couples in debt are considering divorce or bankruptcy as the "solution" to their financial problems.

Unfortunately, as with the previous attempts to avoid the problems rather than deal with them, neither of these "solutions" work either. Statistics tell us that 80 percent of those who get divorced because of financial problems will do so again within three years after remarrying; and about the same ratio of people who go bankrupt will repeat that process.

The reason that most of these "solutions" don't work is that they aren't really solutions; they are symptom treatments. The symptoms are what you see: past-due bills, indulgences, too many credit cards, too large a home, and the like. But the problems are ignorance and attitude. These stem from the violation of some very basic financial principles that are not taught much any more.

It is an indictment of our educational system (and our homes) that people can graduate from high school without even a basic understanding of how to manage money properly. In fact, you can graduate from college with a Ph.D. in mathematics and still not know how to balance a checkbook.

Starting out debt-free is unlikely if you are paying for a home, cars, and a college education. But if you are willing to follow some basic, unchangeable principles that have worked well for hundreds of years prior to this generation, you can become debt-free. Anyone who has the self-discipline to do so can get totally debt-free in three years. Those who purpose to do so can pay off their homes in another seven years, or less.

In this book we will look into the lives of some people who violated these principles and, predictably, wound up deeply in debt. They made the decision to break the cycle that entrapped them and, as a result, became debt-free forever.

We live in an economy that encourages the misuse of credit and then inflicts severe punishment on those who do misuse it. If you don't believe that's true, just talk to anyone who is unable to repay loans offered so freely by lenders—especially credit card lenders. Those same lenders sometimes become downright nasty when they don't get their payments on time.

I trust that this book will put you on the road to financial success and a debt-free lifestyle. If so, you will join a very select group who have found true financial freedom in the midst of the majority, who are little more than financial slaves.

Part One
Three Couples Slide into Debt

1

A National Policy of Growth Through Debt

If you were born after 1950, you don't remember when home mortgages were rare and car loans were for twelve months or less. Prior to that time the local banker was considered the most conservative businessman in town. If someone was approved for a loan, it was generally accepted that he was good for the money. The only regular line of credit most people had was with the local butcher or grocer, and those loans were based on honesty and dependability.

The Great Depression made a lasting impact on millions of people who lost a lifetime of earnings in repossessed farms and mortgages. It also left a lasting impact on lenders, who found themselves in the position of having to repossess homes and farms that were virtually worthless to them. The Great Depression forced Americans to conserve again. Bankers began to make loans only with adequate collateral, and borrowers were extremely cautious because they realized the risks.

But after World War II, the government found itself with several million ex-GIs who needed homes, jobs, and education. With the impact of the Great Depression still fresh in their minds, commercial lenders such as banks and savings and loans were reluctant to extend credit to so many men who had virtually no credit history. So as a last resort, the government became the lender. Congress passed laws allowing the federal government to guarantee loans made to ex-servicemen, and the GI Bill was born. This law allowed commercial lenders to extend credit for education and housing to millions of wartime veterans, and it provided government guarantees to back those loans.

The impact on the economy was immediate and spectacular. Millions of Americans went off to college, and millions more borrowed money to build homes and start businesses. The great credit boom of the twentieth century was off and running. Never before in history had our government used tax-generated dollars to support private lending, but the American people supported the idea whole-heartedly and a new idea was born: consumer credit. Soon the government programs were expanded to provide government-backed loans to non-veterans through the Federal Housing Administration, the Federal Farm Loan Administration, the Small Business Administration, and so on.

With the stimulus of credit feeding the education, housing, and business sectors, prices went up—the natural outgrowth of the law of supply and demand. Credit allowed more people to compete for the available products and services, which in turn allowed prices to increase. Once the cycle began, others were forced to borrow to compete for those items, and private lenders stepped in to provide the loans. The boom of home loans in the fifties provided better housing to young couples at a much earlier age than they could have realized by saving to buy their homes.

But there was a price to be paid, and that price was inflation. Home prices began to creep up in the late fifties, as more and more families entered the market through a wide variety of mortgage options. But as prices climbed, many couples were forced out of the market because they could not afford the monthly payments. The bankers, still leaning to the conservative side, applied the 25 percent rule to housing loans, meaning that no more than 25 percent of the husband's total monthly income could be dedicated to home mortgage payments.

The impasse created by that policy led to a slowdown in buying, not only in the housing industry but also in related industries such as appliances, carpeting, and real estate. A parallel predicament was evident in the automobile industry and in education, both of which had become heavily dependent on consumers' use of loans to buy their products and services. The answer came in the form of longer term loans. By extending the payment period, lenders enabled people with relatively low incomes to afford the monthly payments. Another boom was on.

By the mid-sixties the generation of bankers who had been through the Great Depression was retiring and turning operations over to younger, more aggressive people who had grown up with the debt-oriented mentality. The need to expand the credit base meant that even more loans had to be made available to more people for longer periods of time.

By the seventies virtually every segment of the economy was dependent on credit. Even consumer items such as food, clothing, medical care, and travel were dependent on credit through credit cards and small loans. Lenders extended long-term loans based on equity in assets. Thus consumers could borrow on the appreciated values of their homes, stocks, and businesses. But since the equity was dependent on the availability of loans to subsequent buyers, this created the need for even more lending. The economy was returning to the pre-Depression mentality of growth through debt.

In the seventies the government was no longer just the guarantor of loans. It was the stimulator of massive debt. The economy had become totally dependent on consumers' borrowing to keep it going. The traditional requirements for qualifying borrowers fell by the wayside as lenders sought wider markets for their loans. No longer was the rule in mortgage loans 25 percent of the husband's salary. Now it was 40 percent of both incomes. Car loans were extended to sixty months and often had balloon payments of up to 40 percent at the completion of the loan period.

By the eighties debt had become the engine that fueled the entire economy, and consumers were forced to borrow even the equity out of their homes in order to educate their children and purchase cars. Is it any wonder that, in the midst of this steamroller of debt-financing, the average family experienced financial problems? It is interesting that the increase in the American divorce rate can be tracked on a curve matching the growth of debt in the country. Does the increase in divorce cause the debt to increase, or is it the other way around? I believe that the increased incidence of divorce is a direct result of too much debt. Nearly 80 percent of divorced couples between the ages of twenty and thirty state that financial problems were the primary cause of their divorce.

What can a person do to break out of this cycle? How much credit can an individual or a family handle? These are the fundamental questions that will be addressed in this book.

My intent is twofold. First, I want to help those who are in debt develop a plan to manage their finances. Second, I want to convince anyone that he or she can become debt-free and stay that way, given the desire, discipline, and time.

I believe we are headed for a massive economic recession (or depression), during which the present debt cycle will be reversed. Regardless of what anyone says to the contrary, we cannot continue to run our economy on borrowed money. Eventually the debt burden will become so excessive that even the interest payments cannot be made.

The government is rapidly approaching that point now. Each year it borrows the equivalent of the interest due, even during relatively good economic times.

Consumers and businesses owe nearly $6 trillion in debt, much of it at floating or variable interest rates. Unfortunately, the rates tend to rise when the economy turns sour. Those who are caught in the debt cycle during any major recession quickly discover the meaning of the proverb: "The rich rules over the poor, and the borrower becomes the lender's slave."

2
Sliding Toward a Crisis

Paul and Julie were from middle-income families. They grew up in the suburban area of Chicago and had the normal amount of chores around the house. Julie's father was a realistic person who kept the household records and distributed the money. He gave Julie's mother a housing allowance to manage. He paid all the other bills and gave Julie a strict allowance. Julie was required to work for a portion of her clothing and entertainment money.

In Paul's family the distribution of tasks was different. His mother kept the checkbook and paid the bills. His father never got involved with family finances except when he wanted to buy something. Then he simply wrote a check for the amount he needed. That caused some terrible fights, since he never bothered to write down his check amounts. Paul could almost always go to his dad and get money when he needed it. When he did this, Paul's father usually told him not to tell his mother because she would have a fit. Paul's father worked a great deal of overtime on his job and believed that the money was his to spend as he wished.

Paul held several part-time jobs while he was growing up but rarely stayed at any for longer than a few weeks. The money he made was his to spend as he desired. When he was in the twelfth grade, his father bought him a nice car (on time), and his mother blew up about it because she hadn't been consulted.

When Paul started college, he was encouraged to apply for student aid and government loans. By falsifying the credit reports, he was able to qualify for both. He completed two years of college while living at home but never really decided on a field of study. He took a summer job at a large auto assembly plant and received an offer to stay on permanently, which he accepted.

He and Julie dated for nearly a year after they met in college. When Paul took his permanent job, he asked Julie to marry him, with the understanding that she would complete her education in teaching—a field to which she was very strongly committed.

Neither Paul nor Julie received any detailed instructions from their parents about marriage. It was assumed that the pastor of Julie's church would provide the instruction they needed. Indeed, the pastor did require several hours of counseling on sex, communication, and spiritual values. Once he asked Paul if he would be able to support a family, to which Paul replied, "Yes sir, I'll be making $6.50 an hour at the plant. We'll have plenty of money."

Since that was more than the pastor was making himself (not counting housing or car allowances), he never pursued the subject further. So having completed what they thought were the requirements for marriage, Paul and Julie were married.

Julie read the notice:

Dear Mr. and Mrs. Averal,

Our records show that your VISA account is seriously overdue. We have made numerous attempts to contact you about this matter. This letter is to notify you that your account has been turned over to our Collections Department. You need to clear this account in total to avoid serious damage to your credit rating.

Sincerely,
Robert Bowers, Credit Manager

I don't think I can stand much more of this, Julie thought. *I work hard all day long and then come home to this. There never seems to be enough money anymore. I don't feel like I can ever go out and buy myself a new dress. And now the nursery said they're going to increase Timmy's fees, too.* She groaned. *I wish I were dead.*

Julie truly was convinced that she was at the end of her rope. She resented having to work and felt guilty about leaving her son with strangers every day. She felt trapped.

Meanwhile, Paul was trying to cope with feelings of inferiority and with overwhelming financial pressure. Unfortunately, his method of coping tended to amplify Julie's anxieties.

"Hey, Paul, we're starting the new company bowling league. Are you interested in joining?"

"No, I guess not. I don't know where we'd get the money right now," Paul replied dejectedly.

"Ah, what's the matter, Paul? The wife won't let you have enough to go bowling? Man, I told my wife that I do what I want with my money, and if she doesn't like it, she can find herself another meal ticket."

Maybe that's what Julie is thinking about doing, Paul thought, as he punched out for the day. *It seems that all we ever do anymore is fight about money. I feel awful about our fight last night, but she acted like it's my fault that she has to work. That's so stupid. If she had taken her pills like she was supposed to, she wouldn't have gotten pregnant and we'd be doing fine. Women are supposed to know about those things. I can't help it if she can't go to college now.* But Paul knew his marriage was in serious trouble.

Paul made his way out to his car in the employee parking lot. His stomach felt twisted in knots. He thought about going to a doctor, but the company's insurance plan didn't pay for office visits, and he knew he and Julie didn't have the money.

Paul got into his car and turned the key. All he heard in response was a low growl and then a click.

"Oh nuts," he said as he looked around the nearly empty parking lot. "Now what am I going to do?"

Paul got out of his car and went back into the plant building. He saw one of the second shift maintenance crew and asked if he would help him jump start his car.

"Sure, I'll be glad to, Paul," he replied. "But you need to do something about that old clunker of yours. This is the third time in the last month it wouldn't start."

I wish I could do something about it, Paul thought as they headed out the door. *But we seem to get further behind every month. I had a better car when I was in high school than I do now.*

In a few minutes they had Paul's car started, and he headed home. "Boy, Julie's going to be mad again," Paul said out loud. "This is the second time I've been late this week." Then he thought, *It seems like she's always mad these days. I work as hard as I can, and she keeps nagging about how she always has to do without things. I wonder what she thinks I do?*

As Paul was driving by the Simmon's Auto Sales lot, he saw a sign that read, "Why put up with that old car? We'll put you in a new car for $118 a month, no previous credit necessary."

Paul thought, *I know we can't buy a new car, but it won't hurt to look. I spend more than that on this old pile of junk now, I'll bet.*

An hour later Paul was on his way home, driving a brand new Plymouth. He had signed the contracts but the salesman had assured him that if there was a problem with the car he could trade it back in. Paul was excited to show it to Julie. He knew they could work the $132 a month into their budget. It cost more than the advertised price, but he knew Julie would want an automatic and air conditioning.

As he walked in the door, he could hear the baby screaming. Julie came out of the kitchen. "Paul, where have you been? I could use some help around here. Will you please go and see what's wrong with Timmy? I don't think I can stand his crying another minute." With that she turned back toward the kitchen.

Paul headed into the bedroom to pick up Timmy and snapped, "I don't know what's wrong with you. You're acting worse than a child." Julie did an abrupt about-face and followed him into Timmy's room.

"You're a good one to talk," she yelled with as much anger as she felt inside. "I feel like I've got to take care of two children instead of one. The bank sent me a note at work today about our VISA account. If we don't pay it, they're going to turn it over for collection. If my boss gets another garnishment, he'll probably fire me."

"Ah, that's stupid, Julie. They can't fire you for that. And the bill is not that far overdue anyway."

"So I'm stupid now, too, am I?" Julie shouted as she stormed out of the room. "If I'm that stupid, I guess you should have married somebody else." She slammed the door to their bedroom, and Paul heard the lock click shut.

Depression swept over him as he picked up their son and headed into the kitchen. He didn't know where to turn or what to do. *What would Julie say when she found out about the car?* he wondered. Paul knew she was seriously considering leaving him again. The last time he had been able to talk Julie into coming back, but he knew that she couldn't be talked into coming back if she left this time.

Carrying Timmy with him, Paul went outside and got into the new car. He eased it out of the driveway and drove back to Simmon's Auto Sales. He hoped he could get his old car back without Julie's discovering what he had done. But inside he had the sinking feeling that things were about to get a lot worse.

3
It Didn't Begin Yesterday

When Paul and Julie were married, he was twenty-two and she was twenty-one. They thought they could handle marriage but wanted to delay having children for at least five years. That would give Julie time to finish college and get established in her teaching career. Paul thought he would like to go back to college someday, but not until Julie finished.

But after living in an apartment for five months, Paul decided that it didn't make any sense to keep throwing money away on rent. Some of the guys at work had told him he was losing all the tax breaks the government allowed homeowners. "You're just paying the government's bills for welfare when you rent," another shift worker had said authoritatively. "Get yourself a house and start building some equity." Paul began to look for a home they could buy. He found one that was near their price range, but the bank wouldn't finance it on the basis of his income alone. So during the summer college break Julie took a job as receptionist for a local dentist. Based on their combined incomes, they signed to buy the home. Julie told Paul several times that she didn't think it was a good idea to buy a home, but he assured her that he would be getting raises to cover the additional costs. "Besides," he said, "with the tax breaks we'll get, it won't cost us any more than renting does."

They couldn't afford the down payment, so Paul's dad co-signed for a note at his credit union. Paul neglected to mention the loan on his mortgage application and also failed to mention that Julie's income was temporary. The monthly house payments required almost 60 percent of Paul's take-home pay. Almost immediately they were in financial trouble from the payments alone. With the insurance, taxes, and utilities added, Paul and Julie were on the road to debt without realizing it.

After the first month, Paul was unable to make the loan payment to his company's credit union. When it was sixty days delinquent, the credit union attached his salary and had the payments deducted automatically, as per their written agreement. Paul's father was sent written notice of collection proceedings against him for the two months in arrears. When he received the notice, he hit the roof and stormed over to Paul and Julie's to confront the issue.

By that point, Julie had gone back to school. She had had no knowledge of any financial problems. When she found out, she was devastated. Paul's dad demanded that they pay the past due bill. When Paul told him they could not, his dad suggested that Julie get a job.

"Paul, I can't see any way that we can keep this house," Julie said. "I would rather sell it than drop out of school."

"We won't have to sell the house," Paul replied emphatically. "I can get a loan on my car to catch up the payments. I'm due a raise pretty soon; then we'll have enough to make it."

"I don't know, Paul. What if the raise doesn't come through?" Julie asked.

"You don't need to worry, honey. I take care of the finances in this family. I know it will work out."

With that, Julie put the subject of finances out of her mind. But she couldn't shake the nagging feeling of impending disaster.

Paul negotiated a loan on his car for enough to catch up the credit union payment, with some left over. He used that to buy a VCR, so they wouldn't have to go to the movies, he said. That would save a lot of money. He was sure.

When Paul received his next check with the loan payment deducted, he was shocked. His net pay for the first pay period of the month was just $175. He had already mailed the house payment anticipating his pay, and he realized that the check probably wouldn't clear. Sure enough, he received a note from the mortgage company that his check had been returned for insufficient funds. They demanded immediate payment or they would pursue legal action.

Not knowing what to do, Paul called a local loan company that advertised immediate second mortgage loans for home owners.

"Paul, I absolutely will not sign to get a second mortgage on this house," Julie screamed. "We can't pay the bills we have now!"

"There's nothing else we can do," Paul shouted back. "I have to pay the mortgage or they'll repossess the house."

"I don't care if they do," Julie said, beginning to cry. "I don't think I can take much more of this. I'm going home for a while. I just need to get away and think."

With that, Julie grabbed some clothes and called her mother to come after her. When Julie's dad came home that evening, he asked, "What's the problem, honey?"

"Oh, Daddy, we're in such a financial mess, and I can't get Paul to be honest with me. We seem to get into more trouble every month."

Julie's father was wise enough to call Paul and ask him to come over and talk. Paul explained the problem of the credit union payment being taken out of the first-of-the-month's paycheck, when he thought it would be taken out of the second check. He assured Julie's father that it was all a misunderstanding and that he would be able to make the adjustment the next month.

Rather than allow them to take out a second mortgage, Julie's dad decided to lend them the money himself. He just asked that Paul pay the loan back as soon as he could. Paul assured him that he would do so and that it would be no longer than two months.

Even a casual observer could see at this point that giving Paul and Julie more money was not the answer. But it's often much easier to see the truth in someone else's life than it is in your own. Certainly Paul wasn't trying to deceive anyone. He just didn't have enough information about the way finances worked to make an intelligent decision.

The loan from Julie's father didn't solve any problems. It merely delayed the inevitable. Within two months, bills were backing up again. Creditors were calling day and night to pressure both Paul and

Julie. But most often they wanted to reach Julie because they knew that the wife usually would succumb to pressure more easily than the husband.

It was almost impossible for Julie to concentrate on her school-work. For the first time in her life she began to let her grades slip. That put additional pressure on her, especially when her father called to chide her about her mid-term grades. "Julie, we're sacrific-ing to pay for your books and college tuition, and we expect you to do your part," her father said. "If you don't keep your grades up, we'll stop helping. What's the matter with you? You're capable of doing better work."

Julie was shattered. She had always had the approval of her parents, and now they were putting pressure on her too. An event that very evening became the final straw. She came home from classes at about 6:00 P.M., almost on the verge of tears because of the earlier discussion with her father. She opened the door and flipped on the light switch. Nothing happened. She made her way to the dining room and tried that switch. Still nothing. In another five minutes she knew their power had been turned off.

She grabbed a flashlight and began to look through the desk in their bedroom, where she found two delinquent notices warning that their lights would be turned off if the bill wasn't paid immediately. She also found similar notices from the gas and water companies. She sat there in the dark crying for nearly an hour, until Paul came home.

When Paul came in he said, "Julie, what's the matter with the lights?"

"I'll tell you what's the matter. You haven't paid the bill for the last two months, and they turned our power off. That's what's the matter! And . . . I found notices from the other utilities too. Paul, what's the matter with you? Can't you even keep the utility bills paid?"

"I'm sorry, honey. I intended to pay them but there wasn't enough money in the last paycheck. I'll try to get them caught up next paycheck."

"Oh, Paul, it's always the next paycheck with you. But we never seem to have enough money to catch up. I've decided to quit school and get a job. I just can't live like this anymore."

"I'm really sorry. But I think you're right. If you could just work for a while until we get caught up, it would really help. You should be able to go back next fall. I've got another raise coming that will help a lot then."

Julie quit school and took a typist's job that paid about $700 dollars a month net. For several months things seemed to get better financially, and her relationship with Paul even improved. The extra money allowed them to eat out periodically, and Julie was able to buy a used car so she wouldn't be dependent on Paul to get back and forth to work.

Then Julie began to feel awful in the mornings. When she missed her period, she realized that she might be pregnant. She hadn't been disciplined about taking the birth control pills her doctor had prescribed.

A visit to a local health clinic confirmed her worst fears: she was pregnant. A general feeling of gloom came over her as she thought about Paul's reaction and the fact that not only would a baby curtail her education, but it would also greatly reduce her ability to work. She felt like she was in a box with no way out. She thought briefly about the prospect of an abortion but then put it out of her mind. She could never think of taking a life, especially one that was part of her and Paul. But now she understood the terrible temptation that money pressures created for others who found themselves in the same situation.

"What do you mean, you're pregnant?" Paul shouted when Julie told him. "How could you be so stupid, Julie? All you had to do was take those pills, and you wouldn't have gotten pregnant."

"Do you think I got pregnant on purpose?" Julie screamed back. "I don't like this any more than you do, but there is nothing I can do about it now."

Paul stormed out of their bedroom. Julie collapsed on the bed in tears. She felt guilty about getting pregnant and anxious about the future.

How will we ever be able to pay for a baby? she wondered. *If I stop working, we won't even be able to pay the bills we have now.*

The rest of that evening Julie stayed in the bedroom and Paul stayed downstairs. He began to feel guilty about his reaction to Julie and decided to apologize. But by the time he went upstairs she was asleep.

Julie tried to continue to work, but morning sickness forced her to miss more and more work. Finally her boss called her in to confront the issue.

"Julie, I know you've had a tough time with this pregnancy, but you've missed six days in the last two weeks. We need someone to do your work. Why don't you take a month's leave of absence and stay home? If you're doing better, then come back and see me, and we'll find something for you to do."

"Oh, Mrs. Moore, I can't afford to stay home," Julie replied through a rush of tears. "I have to work, or we can't keep up with our payments."

"Julie, I think that you and Paul ought to consider filing for bankruptcy. You're not going to be able to work while you're so sick. And if you continue the way you're going, you'll ruin your health and the baby's too."

"Bankruptcy? I never thought about it," Julie said. "I thought bankruptcy was only for companies or people who owed millions of dollars."

"No, dear," Mrs. Moore replied. "My husband's firm handles personal bankruptcies all the time. It's certainly no sin to file for bankruptcy anymore. After all, those companies that lend to young couples ought to know better anyway. Talk it over with Paul and give my husband a call if you would like to talk about it. Here's one of his cards."

That evening Julie was quiet through dinner. Paul sensed something new was wrong, but he dreaded asking what it was. Their relationship had been so tense since Julie became pregnant that they rarely spoke to one another without getting into some kind of argument. Finally, he spoke up. "What's wrong now, Julie? You have barely said two words since I got home."

"I lost my job today," she replied matter-of-factly.

"You lost your job!" Paul bellowed as he came up out of the chair. "How did you lose your job?"

"Mrs. Moore said I was taking too much time off, and they needed someone who is more dependable."

"They can't do that. It's illegal," Paul shouted in fear as much as in anger.

"Yes, they can, Paul," Julie replied. "They're willing to give me another job when I can work again. But Mrs. Moore is right. If I keep up this pace, it may be detrimental to the baby's health."

"But what in the world will we do?" Paul said in despair as he sat back down. "We just bought your car, and we can barely make it even when you work."

"Mrs. Moore suggested that we file for bankruptcy protection," Julie replied. "She said her husband handles bankruptcies for couples like us all the time."

"I don't see how that's possible," Paul replied. "Most of our debts are credit cards and department store loans, outside of the house and cars. I don't think you can get out of those debts."

"She said we can," Julie replied, handing Paul the business card Mrs. Moore had given her.

Paul arranged a meeting with the attorney, Joe Moore. "Paul and Julie, I've reviewed your case, and I think I can help you," he said. "Most of your debts are relatively small bills owed to credit card companies and stores. And since you're really in this fix because of an unexpected pregnancy, I believe the judge will grant you a Chapter 13."

"What's a Chapter 13?" Paul asked.

"It's an individual reorganization plan," the attorney replied. "It's set up for cases just like yours when a couple gets into debt over their heads through hardship. The court tells the creditors how much they will receive, based on a plan we submit. Once they receive what the judge allocates, you're cleared of any other liabilities you owe."

"And that's all there is to it?" Paul said in wonderment. "The judge tells them what we can pay, and they have to accept it?"

"That's about it," Mr. Moore replied. "I've seen it help dozens of couples just like you. After all, it's not your fault that Julie can't work anymore. And her company directing her to stay home for at least a month will really help sell this to the court."

"Mr. Moore, I don't feel completely at peace about this," Julie said. "What about the rest of the money we owe? Isn't it our responsibility to pay all of it?"

"Absolutely not. In the first place the creditors carry bad debt insurance to protect them against losses. And second, this law was written to protect young couples like you from abuse by ruthless collection agencies that try to get blood out of a turnip."

We certainly have been harassed by collection agencies, Julie said to herself. "Well, I guess if the law allows it, there is no problem. What do you think, Paul?"

"I think it's the only answer, with you losing your job and a baby on the way."

"Mr. Moore, go ahead with the Chapter 13."

"There's just one more thing. My fee for filing the case will be $450, and you'll need to pay a $50 fee to the court."

"Five hundred dollars?" Paul said in surprise. "We don't have that kind of money."

"Could you get it from your parents?" he asked.

"We've already borrowed from our parents," Julie said. "I don't think any of them would agree to lend us any more."

"That's too bad," the attorney replied. "I need the money up front before I can file the case. There is another alternative, however."

"What's that?" Paul replied.

"Why don't you charge your groceries and utilities on your credit cards for the next month? Then you'll have the money you need. When the bankruptcy takes effect, the charges will be lumped in with the other bills. In fact, it might even help our case because we'll be able to show the judge that your financial situation is getting worse."

"But is that honest?" Julie asked.

"Sure it is," Mr. Moore replied. "Besides, why do you think the credit card companies charge so much interest? They can afford to take a few losses. They're not hurting financially. If you don't believe that, just take a look at their buildings sometime."

"That's for sure," Paul agreed. "Besides, I don't see that we have any alternatives."

Smiling at Julie, Paul said, " Now you'll be able to stay home until the baby's born. By then I'll be making overtime pay again, and you'll be able to go back to school."

"Sound's good," Mr. Moore replied. "I'm always glad to help."

"Thanks, Mr. Moore," Paul said as they got up to leave.

"Sure thing," he replied. "Remember, when the bills come in next month, just put them aside until after the court hearing. Just pay what you have to in order to keep the lights on. But don't put the cash in your checking account, or it will become a part of the assets. Just keep it in your home—somewhere that's safe."

After they left Julie said, "Paul, I don't like the idea of using our credit cards when we know we're not going to pay the bills."

"Listen, Julie, Mr. Moore wouldn't tell us to do something illegal. Besides, what choice do we have? With you pregnant, we can't pay any of the bills anyway. And as he said, the companies can afford the loss. That's why they carry insurance."

4
Things Come to a Head

"Mr. and Mrs. Averal, I've decided to grant your petition for bankruptcy protection in accordance with Chapter 13 of the Federal Bankruptcy Code," Judge Brown said. "You need to understand the conditions of this action. Each month you must meet the minimum payments established in the budget plan you submitted. Failure to do so will constitute a breach of contract and may require this court to remove you from Chapter 13 protection. You will then have to file for personal dissolution under Chapter 7 of the Bankruptcy Code. Do you understand this clearly?"

"Yes sir, we do," replied Paul.

"Very well. But there is one further matter concerning your case that I need to address. There were several charges on your credit cards during the last month prior to filing your petition. Your creditors have requested that these accounts be set aside from this bankruptcy action on the grounds that they were made in contemplation of filing for bankruptcy protection. I have decided to grant their petition as the facts would seem to support that conclusion.

"I want to issue you both a stern warning that this court will not condone or allow such blatant attempts to deceive your creditors. The bankruptcy court is provided to give couples who have had personal financial setbacks beyond their control the chance to start over again. It is not to be used to defraud those who trusted you by extending credit to you.

"I hope you have learned from your bad experiences with the overuse of credit and that you will not repeat the same mistakes. You're young and can reestablish your lives and your credit if you discipline yourselves. The next time, this court will not deal with you so leniently. I set repayment at 50 percent and monthly payments at $100 a month. The court will review your petition in twelve months."

Julie sat in stunned silence. She didn't really hear what the judge said beyond the point where he chastened them for what he concluded to be an attempt to defraud the credit card companies. She realized that was exactly what they had attempted to do. She began to cry as the courtroom cleared.

"What's the matter, Julie?" Paul asked as he and the attorney approached her.

"Oh, Paul, I'm so ashamed of what we tried to do by charging all of our expenses last month while we hoarded our money. Those men from the credit card companies must think we're awful people."

"Don't worry about it, Julie," Joe Moore said. "Our plan worked, and now your total debt payments will be just $100 a month. And with that set aside at 50 percent, you should be totally clear in less than two years."

"I don't understand what 'set-aside' is, Mr. Moore," Paul said.

"It means that you must repay the existing debts up to 50 percent of their current levels, but with no additional interest accumulation."

"You mean we don't have to repay the entire amount?" Paul asked in astonishment.

"No, the judge decided that, based on the petition I made on your behalf, it would be an undue burden on you to repay the entire amount."

"But I think we should repay the entire amount," Julie said. After all, we did borrow the money in good faith. I don't think it would be honorable to repay only half."

"I appreciate your attitude, Julie, but you need to be realistic. You have a baby on the way, and you'll have additional expenses. Don't you think your first responsibility is to your baby?"

"Yes," Julie replied. "But . . . "

"I agree with Mr. Moore," interrupted Paul.

"What's going to happen to the credit card bills we ran up last month?" Paul asked.

"The repayment plan will include those debts each month, but you'll have to repay 100 percent of what's owed. It just means it will take you a little while longer to get out of debt, but it's no big deal. That's always a risk you run when you charge just before a bankruptcy hearing. But I knew the judge wouldn't throw your case out —not with Julie pregnant."

"You mean you knew the judge might not allow the recent charges to be set aside, Mr. Moore?" asked Julie in astonishment.

"Well, I knew it was a possibility. But in this business, nothing ventured, nothing gained. Besides, you're no worse off than you might have been otherwise."

"Only regarding our reputation—that's all," replied Julie as tears welled up in her eyes.

As they headed home Julie commented, "Paul, I don't think we did the right thing. I think we have cheated our creditors."

"I disagree," commented Paul. "It feels like a burden has been lifted off our shoulders. We have a chance to start fresh and get our lives back in order. Wait and see; things are going to work out okay from now on."

As the weeks passed, Julie began to believe that Paul was right. The pressures on their marriage eased as the financial strain from delinquent bills lessened. For several weeks Paul was able to work extra overtime as the plant increased its productivity. They used the extra income to buy baby supplies and the other items Julie would need. She was even able to return to work on a part-time basis, so they had more "free" money than during any previous time in their marriage.

The baby came, and Julie was totally occupied with learning to care for a new infant. Her mother helped until the baby was nearly a month old. Then she returned to her own home.

During the fifth week the baby began to cry more than usual, and Julie took him in for a general check-up. The doctor's diagnosis was colic, a non-life-threatening stomach condition common to many young babies. But as the weeks passed, the baby cried more frequently and eventually began to cry nearly every waking moment. Both Julie's and Paul's nerves began to wear thin.

Paul began to get lax about paying the household bills, and he began to pick up food in the evenings rather than cook at home. The baby took up so much of Julie's time that virtually she was unable to do anything else.

One evening on the way home Paul was involved in a minor automobile accident. He was ticketed and was required to appear in traffic court the next month. He didn't mention the incident to Julie and figured he could scrape together the fine, which he thought would be about $35.

Paul put the incident out of his mind and completely forgot about the court date. Late one evening after arriving home from work he answered the doorbell to find two policemen at his front door.

"Are you Paul Averal?" the older policeman asked.

"Yes, I am, officer," Paul answered. "What can I do for you?"

"Mr. Averal, I have a warrant for your arrest for failure to appear in court to answer charges on a traffic violation and for driving a vehicle without insurance," the officer said.

"Oh no!" Paul exclaimed. "I completely forgot about the ticket. But officer, there must be some mistake. I do have insurance on my car."

"Sir, I would suggest that you get a copy of your policy and come with us. We have a bench warrant for your arrest issued by Judge Simpson. You'll either have to pay the fines assessed or post bail to be released."

"How much are the fines?" Paul asked as Julie came to the door to see what was going on.

"The total is $750, sir," the officer said.

"Seven hundred fifty dollars!" Paul exclaimed. "There must be some mistake. They can't be that much."

"Yes sir, they are," the officer said. "They include a traffic citation, a fine for failure to have liability insurance, and the court and summons charges."

"I know I have insurance," Paul said defiantly. "Wait here, and I'll get a copy of my policy."

Julie began to feel a familiar wave of depression come over her as she heard the conversation. She suspected that the officer was right and Paul was wrong. Her suspicions were confirmed when Paul returned in a few minutes.

"Officer, I found my policy, but it has lapsed. I'm afraid that I forgot to pay the premium. It must have been canceled without their telling me."

"I'm sorry, sir, but you will have to come with us to the station. Your wife can come and post bail in the morning. Then you will need to see the judge about any details."

"How much will the bail be, officer?" Julie asked through her tears.

"It will be the amount of the fines and other charges, ma'am," the officer replied. "But you won't be able to post bail until 9:00 A.M. tomorrow."

"You mean my husband will have to spend the night in jail?" she asked, almost in panic.

"Yes, ma'am," the officer replied. "But he'll be kept in the driver detention cell away from the other prisoners, so don't worry about him. He'll be fine."

With that, they led Paul out to the police car and placed him in the backseat. Julie rushed to the phone and called her father to tell him what had happened.

"Calm down, honey," her father said. "It'll be okay. We'll go down first thing in the morning and get Paul out. In the meantime, why don't you come over here and spend the night with us."

Julie willingly agreed. Her fear and depression were rising to a peak as she thought about the whole cycle of debt and money pressures starting all over again.

The next morning Julie's father put up the money for the bail, and Paul was released. On the way home Julie questioned him about their finances, and Paul confessed that several bills were delinquent.

"There just doesn't seem to be enough money each month," Paul said. "There was for a while, but it seems to evaporate. We just can't make it on my salary, Julie. You're going to have to go to work, especially now that this fine is hanging over our heads. The judge said that I won't be able to drive until the fines are paid and we show proof of insurance."

"But, Paul, we don't have anyone to keep the baby," Julie said as the tears began to flow. She felt like she was in a dark pit with the sides beginning to cave in.

"Maybe we can get your mom to keep him, at least for a while, until we can get some of the bills caught up," Paul said.

"I hate doing that!" Julie screamed. "We're always asking some-one to bail us out of our messes. I wish I had never met you, Paul."

Julie did go back to work and found that she actually enjoyed it. The baby was getting better, and being away from him during the day helped her to cope with the evenings. But soon her mother told her that she could no longer keep the baby. She had a life of her own to lead, and it wasn't fair that she had to raise a second family. Julie cried a lot over the decision but in the end she knew her mother was right, so she started looking for someone to keep the baby. She was shocked at the cost of child care. She finally selected what she thought would be the best child care center, but it would cost her nearly $400 a month.

As the weeks passed, she and Paul continued to argue about money. Julie believed she was a slave to Paul's impulses. He often bought things he wanted—a new television or a CD player—but then there was no money for clothes or eating out. Finally, she decided that she would keep a portion of her paycheck for herself. Instead of bringing the check home as she had in the past, she would stop at the bank and deposit it, taking out the money she needed.

Paul was furious when she told him about it. "Julie, you can't do that," he shouted. "There won't be enough money to pay all the bills."

"Then they will have to go unpaid," Julie yelled back. "I'm not going to worry about it anymore. You never paid my dad back for your fines, and I'm going to start paying him back something every month. Paul, you're a totally irresponsible little boy. I'm sick and tired of working all day and never being able to spend any of my own money."

"Well, if it's your money, why don't you just keep it yourself, and I'll keep my money!" Paul shouted as he stormed out of the room.

"Then I'll do just that," Julie yelled back as he slammed the front door.

Julie spent the next two hours drawing up a budget, dividing their respective expenses. She decided that she should pay for the baby's nursery costs, her transportation, and a fourth of the utilities.

The next day she left work a little early so that she could go to the bank and open a checking account in her name. That evening she informed Paul that she had decided to keep her money and pay her own bills. She handed him a copy of the division of expenses that she had drawn up.

Paul had a sinking feeling inside, as if something had died. And in truth, he knew that something had: their marriage.

"Look, Julie, I'm sorry for what I said last night. I didn't mean it really. I don't want us to have separate checking accounts and split the expenses."

"No, you just want to be able to spend what you want, when you want," Julie spat out. "Well, no more. You pay your part, and I'll pay my part from now on. And if you don't like it, I'll leave."

"Do you really mean that, Julie?" Paul asked with a hurt look on his face.

"I really do," she replied defiantly. "I don't know if I love you anymore, but I do know that I don't respect you. I've been on the giving end of our marriage from the first day. From now on I'm going to do what's best for me."

Paul felt as if someone had just hit him in the stomach with a sledgehammer. *Where did we go wrong?* Paul thought as Julie stormed out of the dining room. *How could I have been so stupid as to let our relationship slip into hatred? I don't know what to do now.*

5

If I Don't Talk About It, It'll Go Away

Paul and Julie Averal are not unique. Perhaps the exact circumstances are different in the lives of other couples, but the end result is the same in millions of marriages throughout America. Like Paul and Julie, most couples start out with the highest expectations for their marriages. Half of them end in divorce —the majority of those because of financial problems.

Unfortunately, few young couples know what they did to create their financial problems or what they need to do to solve them. But before discussing how to solve financial problems, I would like to present the story of another couple. Ron and Sue Hawkins were older than Paul and Julie when they got into financial trouble. But the problems they faced were equally devastating.

Ron was a stockbroker and made an average annual salary of $50,000. He paid the major bills, such as the mortgage payments, car payments, and school bills. He gave Sue a household allowance for necessities, such as food, gas, clothes, and allowances.

Their marriage was a good one, except in the area of finances. Sue sensed that she was not a part of any major financial decisions in either their personal lives or the business where Ron was a participating partner. With their children in school most of the day, Sue would have liked to work part-time in Ron's office, as she did when he first started. However, the other members of the firm did not want their wives involved and established policies prohibiting the involvement of family members in the business.

Over the years, against Sue's counsel, Ron invested sizable amounts of borrowed money in various real estate ventures. He took on potential liabilities as a managing partner in several investments with others in the firm, again against Sue's vehement objections. Sue felt that she had been relegated to the position of a mere child in the family's financial matters, and she resented it greatly.

Then some of the investments in which Ron was involved generated financial problems; and a lawsuit, initiated by a disgruntled investor, threatened to totally destroy their financial worth.

"You know you brought this on yourself," Sue said as Ron read the summons delivered to their home.

"Please, not now, Sue," Ron pleaded, as he lowered his head into his hands. "I feel defeated by this whole thing. I had hoped you would understand."

"Sure, I understand. Your good friends have decided to let you hold the bag for the entire firm," Sue said with an accusing tone. "I told you not to do business with Al Groves. There was something about him I didn't like the first time I met him."

"Oh, spare me the sermon, Sue," he growled. "This has to be the nine hundred and ninety-ninth time you've said that. It's always, 'You never take my advice,' and, 'You never listen to me.' This is serious. Don't you realize how much trouble this can cause me?"

"Can cause *us,* Ron. How much trouble it can cause *us.* That's our main trouble now: you think you're in it alone when it comes to any financial decisions."

"I really don't know what you expect from me," Ron groaned. "I work hard, and I have tried my best to provide a good home for you and the kids."

"I don't care about material things, Ron," Sue replied in a softening tone. "I just want us to be one in our decisions. But you treat me like I'm an idiot when it comes to finances. You listen to everyone else's counsel but mine. Why?"

I just wish I could really be honest with her, Ron thought. *If I could just once share how I feel without her saying "I told you so," or rehashing the past.*

"Ron, when will you finally admit that you don't really want my help?" Sue said as he started to leave the room. "But maybe this time you've gotten yourself in deep enough that you'll admit you actually need it."

Over the next several weeks the financial situation got worse. The disgruntled investor continued to pursue the lawsuit against Ron and his company. And Ron continued to hide most of the facts from Sue, believing that he was sparing her the emotional trauma he was experiencing. But the crisis became both of theirs when Sue read in the local newspaper that all of their property and possessions were listed for possible auction by the district court, pending an upcoming assessment for fraud against Ron.

When Ron came home that evening, Sue was waiting for him. She began to vent the frustration she had been feeling for many years. Not that their marriage was all bad—in many ways they had a better marriage than most, and they had shared many pleasant times together. But Sue had always felt like an observer in their finances, instead of a partner.

She confronted him. "Ron, you told me that lawsuit would amount to nothing, and now I see we have a judgment against us! Is that what you call nothing?"

"I'm really sorry, Sue. I wanted to tell you, but I just didn't know how. The judge decided against us. We lost."

"Lost! I thought you told me there was no validity to the suit at all. How could you have lost?"

"I don't know," Ron said dejectedly. "They even offered to settle when the case began, but my attorney didn't want to because he felt the facts were so obviously in our favor."

"So exactly what does it mean that you lost?" Sue asked, as fear began to well up inside of her.

"It means that we must decide to file for bankruptcy, or they will take our home and everything else. I don't want to go bankrupt. I know I've done a lot of foolish things. I'm just sorry that I didn't listen to you or let you be a part of the decisions."

"I have to be honest, Ron," Sue said with tears in her eyes. "I'm really scared too, but if this brings us closer together, I wouldn't have it any other way. I don't believe that we should choose bankruptcy."

"But, honey, it may well mean that we'll end up totally broke after ten years of marriage."

"Ron, I don't care about that. You and I were closer when we had nothing than we are now." Sue walked over and put her arms around him.

6

If Only the Baby Had Been Well

Jack and Mary Thompson each took a teaching position with the same school in the South after they graduated from college. They met while on staff there, fell in love, and got married.

Jack and Mary both came from good homes, but were from very different economic backgrounds. Mary's father was a successful dentist, and although he was not wealthy by any means, he made a very comfortable living. Mary was not indulged as a child, and she was expected to work to help pay her way from her teenage years on. Her college tuition was provided by her parents but she was required to work summers to earn money for her books, clothes, and incidentals, which she did.

Jack came from a much more modest background. His mother and father were divorced when he was nine years old. His mother struggled financially after the divorce, and money was always in short supply in his home. He received a scholarship to attend college and worked long hours to pay his expenses while he was there.

Jack and Mary had been married two years when they had their first child. The school they worked for paid low salaries, and they had been unable to accumulate any significant savings. But they did have what seemed to be an adequate insurance plan, so they thought they would be all right financially. The baby would be born during their summer break, so Mary would be able to work right up to the time of the birth.

There were two things that they hadn't planned on. One was that Jack's salary alone was too low to meet their minimum needs, regardless of how much they scrimped; and two, that the baby would have major health problems. He was born with spina bifida and required constant attention. The initial hospital bill was more than $20,000, with their deductible portion being almost $8,000.

Within six months of the baby's birth they were in debt for nearly $12,000 and sinking further behind every month. When they attempted to pay any portion of the doctor or hospital bills, they fell behind on payments for their monthly living expenses. If they tried to keep up on their living expenses, they fell behind on their medical bills.

By the seventh month some of the accounts had been turned over to collection agencies, and Mary was getting frequent, often rude, calls at home. She was an emotional wreck and her pediatrician, who was also a friend, suggested that Jack consider filing bankruptcy to relieve some of the financial pressure.

Coming home from the doctor's office Mary asked, "What did you think about what Doctor Reese said?"

"I don't know, Mary. I've always believed that you should pay your bills, but that seems to be impossible in our case. Every month we get further behind in our bills. What do you think?"

"I don't know the answer, either. But I do know I can't live under the kind of pressure I feel right now. We can't pay the doctor or hospital bills anyway, so I don't see what difference it would make if we file for bankruptcy. If we're ever able to pay, we can always start repaying the bills, can't we?"

"I guess so," Jack replied. "I don't feel at peace about it, but I honestly don't know of another alternative. I'll call Bill Johnson, an attorney in the civic club I meet with on Mondays, and ask if he handles cases like these. But we don't even have the money it takes to file for bankruptcy unless he'll agree to take his fee in installments."

7
Three Personal Traits that Lead to Debt

How did Paul and Julie, Ron and Sue, and Jack and Mary get into debt? They did so through three avenues: ignorance, indulgence, and poor planning.

IGNORANCE

Paul and Julie represent the majority of young couples today. They enter marriage with little or no understanding of finances and quickly find themselves overwhelmed by the opportunities they encounter to spend more than they make. Since opposites do attract, usually one partner is an optimist, who generally looks toward the future to straighten out any errors in the present. The other is a worrier, who needs stability and security. The optimist doesn't purposely lie to his spouse. He convinces himself that things will change for the better. Paul was an optimist.

Julie, the worrier, became suspicious of Paul because of what appeared to be deceptions and financial irresponsibility. She was forced to drop out of school and give up her career plans, for which she blamed Paul. Then the additional pressure of an unexpected baby added to their financial problems, plus the fact that he was a screaming, colicky child. So Julie developed great hostility.

After counseling a multitude of couples in circumstances nearly identical to Paul and Julie's, I think I can say with some degree of certainty that the financial situation in which they found themselves was indicative of their lack of training and knowledge. They were not stupid—just ignorant. Julie's rebellion could be the subject for an entire book. It was fed by unrealistic and unbiblical desires for self-fulfillment. Apparently she had been taught that her worth as a woman was dependent on attaining a college degree and developing a career outside the home.

Paul, on the other hand, was living in a dream world all his own and angering his wife as he did so. He refused to take responsibility for his decisions and tried to blame their problems on Julie. If she went to work, their problems would be solved. If she had taken her pills, she wouldn't have gotten pregnant. Paul tried to shift the blame to her and sneak around behind her back with his personal indulgences.

A weak-willed man is often attracted to a strong-willed woman. If such a man doesn't take his responsibilities seriously, his wife will be forced to assume the role of authority in the home. Taken to the extreme, the husband and wife will usually end up right where Paul and Julie were—she'll be the decision maker and he'll be the wimp.

INDULGENCE

Indulgence, impulse buying, and get-rich-quick schemes all have the same root cause: greed. Most of us don't like to hear that because we're all prone to at least one of those problems. In reality, they are just different levels of the same basic problem. Ron suffered from a get-rich-quick mentality that manifested itself in his taking excessive investment risks. His wife, Sue, could have provided a balance, but he excluded her from decisions involving money.

Ron indulged himself through his investments, just as another person might through the purchase of expensive cars, houses, or jewelry. Each of us has special indulgences that stem from an attitude of lust. Lust is not limited to the area of sex. In our society more people may lust after power and wealth than after sex.

Often we have the mistaken idea that more money will solve our financial problems. Ron—and others like him—is living proof that more money can easily result in bigger problems. Men who invest in high-risk deals that fail often transfer the blame to other people. Since the family is the most readily available scapegoat, they are the ones who usually receive the blame. "I was doing it to better provide for my family," the man says. Nonsense. He did it because it fed his ego and it was a chance to get rich quickly.

POOR PLANNING

At first glance, it appears that Jack and Mary fell into financial difficulty through no fault of their own. And that is true to some extent. Who could have predicted the problems they had with their first child? Most of us could not handle the expenses created by the medical treatment the child needed. But even without those extraordinary medical expenses, eventually Jack and Mary would have had financial problems anyway. Why? Because their break-even point was beyond Jack's income. Without Mary's working, they simply couldn't make it. The child's medical expenses just made a bad situation impossible.

The symptom they faced was debt, but the real problem was poor planning. They had never been trained in finances and did not know how to establish a budget. Jack took a teaching position that did not have the potential to meet the most basic needs of his family, at least without Mary's income. So the expenses they faced because of the baby did not cause their financial difficulties—they merely amplified them.

Part Two

Three Couples, and a Fourth, Climb Out of Debt

8
Debt and Borrowing

We have seen how three different couples got into debt. Now we need to examine how they got out of debt, because ultimately each of them did. Their marriages survived because the couples were willing to work together and to do the things required to put their financial affairs in order, no matter how difficult they were.

But before we examine how these couples got out of debt, we need to look at some principles concerning debt and borrowing because much of the counsel on debt in this book is based on those principles.

PRINCIPLES OF DEBT

PRINCIPLE 1: THE DEBTOR IS IN SERVITUDE
TO THE ONE WHO LENDS TO HIM

Debt is not a well-understood term today. Most people use the word *debt* to describe any borrowing, but although that is not entirely inaccurate, it is not precise enough.

Let's look at the conditions of indebtedness. Even if a debt is current (all payments up to date), the borrower is potentially in a position of servitude. But if the debt is delinquent, the lender is given an implied authority. Many years ago that authority extended to imprisonment, slavery, and the confiscation of a borrower's total worldly possessions. While that may seem extreme, there is no doubt that the lender has a legitimate right to recover what has been lent. To say the least, borrowing was *not* a decision to be taken lightly.

Here in America—even in the twentieth century—lenders have forced the imprisonment of a borrower who failed to pay back what was owed. Almost any major city library still has records from a debtors' prison. I found several good examples from the turn of the century in Atlanta. One record read, "Abraham Johnston, white male, commended to debtors' prison for a period of six years, or until the debt is resolved, for failure to pay the agreed-upon sum of $200 for the purchase of a mule." Another read, "Sara Wright is sentenced to debtors' prison for an indefinite period of time for habitual indebtedness." The sentence went on to describe her despicable crimes, such as charging food that she couldn't pay for at a merchant's store, charging dry goods at a department store, and signing for a loan with a local citizen without the ability to make restitution.

It is evident that our attitudes today about debt and those of our predecessors were somewhat different. The cause for the difference can be pinpointed as greed and indulgence. Not on the part of the borrowers—that came later. The initial greed was on the part of elected officials who desired to expand our economy by way of debt. To do so required a drastic alteration of the rules regarding borrowing and the consequences of failure to repay.

Few people today are willing to risk forfeiting their freedom and separation from their families to borrow money. The risk would simply be too great. So the laws were amended to make borrowing less risky and credit more available. And besides, who would tolerate the government's borrowing massive amounts of money that could not be repaid while friends and relatives languished in debtors' prisons for failure to repay their personal loans?

The old laws for delinquent debts seem harsh and unnecessarily cruel to us today, and perhaps they were. But the principles behind them were sound and just. The laws assumed that nobody was forced to borrow money—people borrowed money voluntarily. The lender extended honor (money), and the borrower represented himself as trustworthy. Thus the punishment for defaulting on a debt was actually more severe than for theft because it was considered a breach of trust.

PRINCIPLE 2: BORROWING IS PERMITTED

Since I began teaching principles of handling money in 1973, many books have been written and seminars taught on the subject. Some well-intentioned teachers have taken the position that all borrowing is prohibited and that, consequently, no one should be involved in any borrowing or lending.

I wish it were that simple, but it isn't. When I first came across this prohibition in my study on finances I thought, "Aha! Here is the justification for us to get rid of all credit, especially those who have misused it." But I found myself in a quandary. I'd like to share my conclusions, for I believe them to be accurate and confirmed. You can make up your own mind. Just bear in mind that when I began my study I was looking for a justification of the teaching that all borrowing is wrong.

PRINCIPLES OF BORROWING

From time to time an overzealous teacher will present principles as if they were laws. They are not. A *principle* is an instruction to help guide our decisions. A *law* is an absolute. Negative consequences may follow from ignoring a principle, but punishment is the likely consequence of ignoring a law.

An example from our society is driving and drinking. A good rule, or principle, to follow is never to drink. But the law says that if you drink and drive, you'll lose your license and perhaps go to jail.

The *principle* of borrowing is that it is better not to go surety on a loan. *Surety* means that you have taken on an obligation to pay without a specific way to pay it. If you ignore the principle of borrowing, you can be in constant jeopardy.

The *law* of borrowing is that it is wrong to borrow and not repay. Keep in mind there is a difference between the person who *can* repay but will not and the one who *wants* to repay but *cannot*.

PRINCIPLE 1: DEBT IS NOT NORMAL

Regardless of how it seems today, debt is not normal in any economy and should not be normal. We live in a debt-ridden society that is now virtually dependent on a constant expansion of credit to keep the economy going. That is a symptom of a society whose value system is weak sometimes concerning issues such as abortion, pornography, and adultery. People who would never think of participating in those areas do fail to set high standards in the area of credit.

PRINCIPLE 2: DO NOT ACCUMULATE LONG-TERM DEBT

It's hard to believe that a typical American family accepts a thirty-year home mortgage as normal today, or that it is now possible to borrow on a home for nearly seventy years. That's correct—it is not a misprint—seventy years. The need to expand the borrowing base continually forces longer mortgage loans. Why? Because expansion through taking on debt causes prices to rise through inflation. As prices rise, mortgages lengthen.

Inflation is a reflection of the expansion of the money supply via borrowed money. For example, the average home in America sells for about $108,000 (late 1991). Since the average income in America is only about $26,000 (by the most generous measure), those two averages just don't compute. Today it requires nearly 70 percent of the average family's total income to buy the average home, even with a thirty-year mortgage. But what is that average home really worth? To determine that, assume that homes could no longer be sold using long-term mortgages. How much would the average home sell for if it could be bought with cash only? Certainly not for $108,000. It would probably sell for between $20,000 and $25,000. All of the additional cost is inflation created through the use of long-term debt.

How can new home loans be made for up to seventy years? It is done by creating a loan based on a thirty-year amortization schedule but using a seven-year loan period. Thus, the loan must be renegotiated every seven years. Continuing that cycle to pay off the home makes the effective loan period approximately seventy years.

PRINCIPLE 3: AVOID SURETY

By now you understand that surety means accepting an obligation to pay without having a certain way to make that payment. The most recognizable form of surety is co-signing for the loan of another. But surety also can be any form of borrowing in which you sign an unconditional guarantee to pay.

The only way to avoid surety is to collateralize a loan with property that will cover the indebtedness, no matter what. Many home buyers think that because they buy an appreciating asset, such as a home, they are safe from surety. That is not so. In most states a lender can sue to collect a deficit on a home mortgage in the event of a default. And remember that most defaults happen during a bad economy, when the prices of homes are most likely to drop.

Credit card purchases have become the most common form of surety in our generation. In this transaction one merchant sells you the material and another finances the purchase (except for in-store credit cards). In the event of a default, the return of the merchandise does not cancel the debt because the finance company has no interest in the merchandise.

PRINCIPLE 4: THE BORROWER HAS
AN ABSOLUTE COMMITMENT TO REPAY

In this generation, situation ethics is widely accepted, so it is easy to rationalize not paying a debt, especially when the product or service is defective or when one's financial situation seems to be out of control, as with the third couple, Jack and Mary. Both the divorce rate in America and the number of bankruptcies attest to the fact that we are a situational society. The media present unrealistic expectations of what a marriage should be like, and the "me" generation expects individual rights to be totally upheld in a marriage. When those unrealistic expectations fail to materialize, about half of all spouses call it quits.

The same can be said of those who borrow money. The easy access to credit today leads many people to believe that paying their debts will be a snap. Unfortunately, many borrowers discover that it is possible for them to accumulate far more debt than they can repay and still maintain the lifestyle they want. As a result, they bail out. Every year about 500,000 choose bankruptcy as a way to avoid repayment. Yet the average indebtedness for couples in bankruptcy is only about $5,000.

As the attorney for a couple in bankruptcy said, "Bankruptcy must be okay, or the government wouldn't allow it." That is true only if you assume that government in America today follows strong principles, which is hardly true.

Voluntary bankruptcy is an act by a borrower to avoid his or her creditors. In some situations a voluntary bankruptcy is acceptable, but only in the context of trying to protect the creditors—never in the context of trying to avoid repayment.

Signing your name to a credit slip is the same as making a vow to pay that amount of money. So, if you are careful what vows you make, voluntary bankruptcy won't be necessary.

9
Learn to Face Reality

How did Paul and Julie Averal get themselves out of debt? It took hard work and a commitment to follow some basic principles concerning the handling of money.

Paul realized that he had placed his marriage in great jeopardy and that Julie was poised to leave at any time. She had left before over disputes concerning money, but had returned when Paul promised he would not repeat his mistakes. It was entirely likely that Julie would not return if she were to leave again.

Several times in the past Julie had asked Paul to call a financial adviser and set up an appointment for counseling. Paul had always refused. And he always had the promise of more income just around the corner that would solve their problems. But after Julie opened her own checking account, it was Paul who asked her if she would go to the financial adviser with him. She flatly refused.

Nobody is going to be able to help our marriage, Julie thought as she drove out of the driveway one morning not long after she had set up the new bank account in her name. *It really is finished. But why? Do I still love Paul?* she wondered. *I don't know. Our whole married life has been one continual struggle over finances.*

All day she thought about her options and silently prayed. As far as she was concerned, her marriage was finished; she didn't know what she was going to do. She had purposely opened her own checking account so that she could accumulate some funds if, and when, she went out on her own. But she knew she didn't make enough money to pay for child care, a house, a car, and other expenses. She was shocked by her own thoughts. She had actually been planning to leave Paul. Then she realized that it was not a divorce she wanted. She wanted to be free of the pressures they had been facing since the day they got married. Paul was a good man, and she believed he loved her. It was just that he was so irresponsible in the area of finances.

That evening Julie found Paul already home and preparing supper in the kitchen. "Paul," she said in genuine astonishment, "why are you home so early? Is anything wrong at work?"

"No," Paul said without looking up. "I just realized that because of my stupidity I have lost something very precious to me. Julie, it's not more money I need. I need help. I called Pastor Rhimer today and explained what a mess I've made of our finances and our marriage. The pastor is willing to work with me on the marriage, but he recommended a financial counselor in the church to help with our finances."

"Paul, I think that's great," Julie said with enthusiasm.

"But the financial counselor won't meet unless we both go. I didn't know what to tell him," Paul said with tears in his eyes.

"Call and tell him we'll be glad to meet," Julie said as she gave Paul a big hug. "I just hope there is a way out of the mess we're in."

The next day Paul and Julie went to the counselor, Bob Woods. Before he met with them, he asked them each to complete a short personality test. When they were finished with the test, he called them into his office.

Mr. Woods said, "Paul, tell me what you think the problems are."

Paul was taken aback by the question. He had expected Mr. Woods to ask to see the multitude of records they had brought with them. "I honestly don't know," Paul answered. "I suppose it has to be my handling of the money. We never seem to have enough to pay all the bills. We still owe Julie's dad for most of the loan he made to reinstate our car insurance. We owe for two cars, a consolidation loan with the credit union, and our house."

"Thanks, Paul," Mr. Woods said. "Julie, what do you think the problems are?"

"Well, I guess it's much like Paul said, except that I believe the real problem—at least in our marriage—is that we don't discuss things. We argue, and I see it getting worse instead of better."

"Are you willing to make the changes necessary to cure the problems rather than just treat the symptoms?" Mr. Woods asked.

"I'm ready to do whatever I have to do," Paul said.

"I think I am, too," agreed Julie. "But is this going to be one of those lectures on wives obeying their husbands and being silent in the home?"

"I certainly don't think so," replied Mr. Woods. "You two are to operate as a team. I generally find that the wife brings a needed perspective to the finances. But the specific problems must be dealt with first. Then we'll decide who should do what. I need to get an idea about where you are financially right now. So I'm going to ask you some questions, Paul. Feel free to speak up, Julie, if you think Paul has missed anything or you have some input."

With that, Mr. Woods took out one of his budget work sheets and started down the list of monthly expenses. Paul gave most of the answers, but when it came to regular expenses, such as those for clothes, food, laundry, and child care, he deferred to Julie's better memory.

When they had completed the list, Mr. Woods began to list their outstanding debts. Paul was noticeably hesitant once they had gone through the obvious debts, such as the house mortgage, credit union loan, car loans, and family loans.

"What's the problem, Paul?" Mr. Woods asked, sensing that Paul was holding back.

"I need to tell you something," Paul said hesitantly. "But I'm afraid Julie will really get upset if I do."

"Paul, I can't help you unless I know all the facts," Mr. Woods said. "If you owe something else that's not reflected in our records, you need to let me know about it."

"Well, about two months ago when Julie and I were having a lot of problems, I bought a new car," Paul confessed.

"You bought a new car!" Julie exclaimed. "How did you buy a new car? And where is it? I've never seen it."

"Julie, give Paul a chance to explain," Mr. Woods said. "He is trying to be honest with you now."

"I bought the car from a local dealer with the understanding that I could return it if Julie wanted me to. When I got home, we had a big fight about our VISA account being turned over to a collection agency. So, without telling Julie, I tried to return the car, and I found that the dealer wanted $650 to take it back."

"Paul, how could you do that without even asking me?" Julie said with anger in her voice.

"Wait a minute, Julie. Let Paul explain. What's done is done. Let's try to work this out," Mr. Woods said calmly.

"Julie, I know it was stupid and I should have asked you, but our old car was constantly breaking down and I stopped to look at new cars and, well, the salesman did say I could return it. He didn't mention anything about a restocking fee."

"Where does the car loan stand now, Paul?" Mr. Woods asked.

"I signed a note for the $650 so they would take the car back. Now they're threatening to sue me if I don't pay up. But I don't know where the money will come from, Mr. Woods."

"Okay, a $650 note due and payable," Mr. Woods noted on his sheet. "Anything else?"

"One thing," Paul replied as he looked over at Julie and saw her grimace. "I owe $500 on our VISA for a car stereo I bought about a month ago."

"I thought you saved the money to buy that stereo from your overtime pay," Julie said.

"I did, but I also bought an equalizer and some new speakers, plus there was an installation fee. It all came to nearly $500, and I didn't have the extra money so I charged the whole thing."

"What happened to the money you had for the stereo?" Mr. Woods asked.

"I kept it, planning to use that to pay the VISA bill," Paul replied. "But somehow it all was spent before the bill came."

"So now we owe another $500 on the VISA?" Julie shouted as the tears welled up in her eyes.

"Julie, please calm down," Mr. Woods said in a gentle voice. "We knew the situation was bad or you wouldn't have come here.

But I appreciate Paul's honesty about the debts. I can't be of any help to you if I don't know the entire situation.

"As I see it, you have some pressing debts that have to be dealt with rather quickly. Paul, when you elected to file the Chapter 13 bankruptcy you made an agreement not to incur any additional debts until the three-year payment period expired. Now you have an additional $1500 in debt that the court doesn't know about. The first thing you need to do is deal with that situation. I assume you don't have any surplus funds that can be used to pay these bills, do you?"

"No sir," Paul replied. "Only what's in the checking account, which isn't much right now."

"You'll need that for normal living expenses," Mr. Woods said. "Do you have any surplus in your account, Julie?"

Julie sat silently for several moments before she spoke. "Yes, I do, Mr. Woods. But I don't want to use it to pay for Paul's indulgences."

"I can understand that," Mr. Woods said. "But if you're going to work out this situation and find a permanent solution, it will be because you do it together, working as one unit. If you're holding the money as a nest egg, in case the marriage doesn't work out, it won't."

"But Paul doesn't take the leadership in our home," Julie protested. "So am I supposed to turn over all the money to him knowing that it will be spent foolishly?"

"No," Mr. Woods replied. "The way to balance one extreme is not to go to another. You need the balance that each offers the other. You must work together as one.

"Anyone can help you manage the money and pay the bills. That's a matter of following a plan I'll outline for you. But the financial problems you have are really symptoms of greater problems that exist. So unless you deal with the root problems, the symptoms will always return.

"In marriage a man and woman become one. No couple can keep their assets separated and be one. There are some risks when you totally surrender your rights, but there are are also some big rewards.

"Julie, I can't tell you what to do. All I can do is offer you counsel based on what I think you and Paul should do. I want you each to think about your situation. Call me when you have made a decision, and we'll get back together.

"In the meantime, Paul, I want you to call the bankruptcy court's trustee, Mr. Helms; give him the facts, and let him know that we're working together. Mr. Helms and I have communicated many times so, if he has a question, tell him to call me. Also, I want you to contact the manager of the bank that holds the note on your car and tell him that we're working out a plan and will be in contact with him in the next two weeks. But you'll have to pay at least the minimum on the VISA bill, or your Chapter 13 plan will be in jeopardy."

During the next few days Julie hardly spoke to Paul. He tried to be as helpful as possible by doing things around the house and taking Timmy on walks in the evenings.

Julie found herself in a total state of confusion during the week. She had separated herself from Paul financially, if not physically. She considered what Mr. Woods had said about their problems. Inside she knew he was right.

Finally, she made the decision to cross the invisible line back into her marriage and work at becoming one with Paul. She also knew that she had to give up her personal goals of finishing college and having a career. She would work at her marriage and learn to be content.

Suddenly she felt free—as if a great burden had been lifted from her shoulders. She could hardly wait to get home to tell Paul about her decision.

She arrived home before Paul and was sorting through the mail when she came across an official-looking envelope from the Internal Revenue Service. Her stomach did such a flip that she thought she might throw up. She sank down in one of the dining room chairs. She just stared at the envelope for several minutes. She wasn't sure she even wanted to know what it said. She suspected that Paul hadn't filed their taxes or that they were being audited.

She stood up, took a deep breath, and started to open the envelope. *No,* she thought, *I'll wait and let Paul open it. We'll face whatever it is together.* She dropped the letter on the table and began to fix their dinner.

Paul came home a few minutes later and walked over to where Julie was preparing dinner.

"Hi, honey, how did your day go?" Paul asked cheerfully.

"My day went great," Julie replied as she wiped her hands and hugged Paul's neck.

Paul was shocked by her sudden display of affection. It had been several months since she had even kissed him voluntarily. Their physical relationship had deteriorated to the point where Paul was afraid to show any affection, for fear she would totally reject him.

"Paul, I know I've been depressed and moody about our finances the last few months," Julie confessed.

"Don't worry about it, honey," Paul replied. "I've given you plenty of cause to be worried in the past. But I am committed to making a change. I want our marriage to work."

"Hush, Paul, and let me say what I want to say first. It doesn't matter about the problems anymore. We'll work them out together as long as you'll let me help. I have decided to close out my checking account and put the money into our joint account. I have about $500 in savings, and I want you to use it to pay off some of the debts."

"Honey, I can't let you do that," Paul protested. "That money is yours. It seems like somebody else always has to clean up my messes."

"No, you're wrong. The money is not *mine*," Julie said emphatically. "It is *ours*. And I want the money in my account to be used for *our* expenses."

They just stood there several minutes holding each other. Then Julie said, "Paul, a letter came from the IRS today. I didn't want to open it, so I left it on the table."

"Oh no, what now?" Paul said as he picked up the envelope from the table. "I know we don't owe any money to the IRS. At least I certainly hope we don't."

Opening the envelope Paul let out a whoop. "Julie, we don't owe any money! This is a check for nearly nine hundred dollars."

"Why did they send us a check?" Julie asked as she began to relax her body from the shock she had expected.

"Let's see, the letter says that we overpaid our taxes because of an error in computation. At least my math errors worked in our favor this time. Honey, with this we'll be able to pay off the debts and still have some of your money left. Let's go out and celebrate tonight."

"No way," Julie responded. "That's the kind of thinking that got us into this mess in the first place."

"Just kidding," Paul said with a big grin. "I would much rather stay home and celebrate with my family."

Two weeks later Paul and Julie were back in Mr. Woods's office. "Well, Paul and Julie, I'm really glad to see you back again," he began. "Obviously your presence here means you have decided to work together on your financial problems. I'll be honest with you. About half of the couples who come to me don't ever come back. They are looking for either a guaranteed miracle or some kind of quick fix. But if you didn't get into debt in three months, you won't get out of debt in three months."

"Mr. Woods, we're not looking for a miracle or a quick fix," Paul said. "I know I created this mess by my own ignorance and childishness. I'm willing to do whatever is necessary to solve this once and for all."

"What about you, Julie?" Mr. Woods asked.

"I'm committed to whatever it takes," Julie said confidently. "I have already closed my personal account and put the surplus in our joint account."

"Good for you! I believe Paul is going to be worthy of your trust. Now let's get down to business.

"Your combined incomes are approximately $2400 a month. Is that right?"

"Yes," Paul replied. "That's pretty close."

"And your net take-home pay is about $1800?"

"I don't really know," Paul replied.

"Yes it is," Julie chimed in.

"Okay," Mr. Woods said. "I calculate your overall housing expense to be about $1000 dollars a month. That means it takes nearly 55 percent of your total spendable income just to maintain your home. That's at least 15 percent too high for your income. Housing should never cost more than 40 percent of your spendable income."

"I was convinced all along that our home cost us too much," Julie said. "But I didn't know how to calculate what we could afford. The bank used 25 percent of our total incomes when we bought the house. But I was making more money then."

"Gross income doesn't mean a thing," Mr. Woods said. "It's what you have left over to spend that's important."

"Are you saying that we should sell our home and move to a cheaper one?" Paul asked.

"I'm not going to tell you to do anything," Mr. Woods replied. "I'm just going to point out some logical alternatives. Then you'll have to make your own choices. I know that usually the wife is attached to her home, and giving it up is a difficult decision."

"Not for me," Julie said quickly. "I have always viewed that house as an anchor around our necks. It was Paul who really wanted it in the first place."

"That's probably true," Paul said. "But the guys at work said it was stupid to pay rent when I could buy a home and get all the tax breaks."

"Usually that's pretty good logic, but not when you wreck your budget to buy. It would be better to rent and stay within your income than to buy and end up in debt," Mr. Woods said. "I believe you could potentially free up $400 a month by renting for a while."

"Four hundred dollars a month!" Paul exclaimed. "Why that's enough to pay our obligations and more. I guess I never realized the house was putting us into debt, Mr. Woods. I always thought of it as a good long-term investment."

"For most families it is, Paul. But only after they have settled into a lifestyle and found a home within their budget. Buying a home too quickly and one that is too expensive is the number one reason most young couples end up in financial trouble. And since about 50 percent end up in divorce, the home will eventually be sold anyway."

"But why doesn't someone tell young couples those things before they make the mistakes we made?" Julie asked.

"Because, unfortunately, in our society people make money off the excesses of others."

"I never heard that before," Paul said in amazement. "I'll put the house up for sale today."

"Hold it just a minute, Paul," Mr. Woods said. "Don't do anything in haste. You need to think about some other areas, too. I'm going to give you a workbook that will help you to plan each area of your budget. It's especially important that you allocate money for non-monthly expenses such as clothes, car maintenance, and annual insurance. Those are normally areas that create crises when they are due."

"That's certainly true in our case," Julie said.

"We want your budget to be totally realistic, or it will only work a short while. You're going to be tight on money for another year and a half, until your past debts are paid. But with some discipline, you will be debt-free in less that two years.

"I have one additional recommendation for you. I believe Julie is far better equipped to maintain the records and pay the bills. The short personality test I gave you last time shows that she is a detail person, while you, Paul, are a generalist."

"I would agree with that," Paul said. "But I have always been taught that it is the man's responsibility to run the finances in his family."

"Paul, each of us has gifts and abilities to help us in our daily lives. It's clear that Julie is better suited to be the bookkeeper in your family. That doesn't alleviate your responsibility to oversee your family's finances. The two of you together need to work out a financial plan, and then she will pay the bills and maintain the records. In this way you'll be working as a team with your different and unique abilities to enhance the relationship.

"Our short-term goal will be to get your finances to the point where you're able to pay everyone what you owe them each month. That means Julie will need to continue to work, at least for a while. But our long-term goal will be to free you financially so that Julie does not have to work."

"But, Mr. Woods, we have tried that before. Every time I quit working we fell further and further behind," Julie said.

"That's because you started out with expenses larger than your income. I believe you'll find when you readjust your budget that you'll be able to get by on one income. Later, if you want to work, you should use your income for one-time purchases."

"What do you mean?" asked Paul.

"Save it up and buy a car, or save it for a down payment on a home. But don't commit yourselves to monthly expenses based on two incomes, especially at your age. If you do, something as normally exciting as a child can end up being the source of grief and conflict."

"That's for sure," Paul replied, looking at Julie.

"I want you both to go home with the plan I have given you and make the necessary adjustments in your budget. Remember that each and every category of spending must have some money allocated to it. To ignore areas like entertainment and recreation is unrealistic and will cause your budget to fail within a short period of time. Ignoring needs like clothing, auto repairs, and dental bills will make your budget look good but will also make it totally unrealistic.

"You made an agreement with the court to pay your creditors according to the budget you submitted, so you must do so. I believe you will honor your word now that your attitudes have changed. Good luck to you!".

10

Develop and Carry Out a Plan for Paying Off Debts

I trust that by now you recognize the errors that Paul and Julie made in their finances. Their problem could be called "too much, too soon." It is a common malady for many young couples in our society. It has been said (and unfortunately is all too true) that a young couple today tries to accumulate in three years what their parents took thirty years to accumulate. The one thing couples need to learn very quickly is that individuals must be self-disciplined today. They cannot count on the lenders to force them to live within their means, as they once did.

Prior to the late sixties, bankers were among the most conservative people in our society. Before anyone could borrow for consumables such as food or clothes, or even for non-consumables such as cars and houses, his financial status was thoroughly reviewed, and formulas were applied to ensure his borrowing stayed within his means to repay. That is not true today. The increasing demand to make more loans has widened the parameters of acceptable loans. It is now assumed that the borrowers will discipline themselves to repay what they borrow. Unfortunately, many young couples have no idea how to calculate what they can or cannot afford to pay.

More than 60 percent of all first-time home loans require two salaries to make the payments. But since the vast majority of first-time home buyers are couples under thirty-five years old, the prospect of a baby disrupting their cash flow is almost a certainty. So they have built-in potential financial problems from the outset. Combine that with the use of second mortgages—to help make the down payments and loans for refrigerators, lawn mowers, and curtains—and you can see why so many young couples end up in financial trouble.

But the main purpose of this book is not to show how most people get into debt but rather to help you understand how to get out of debt. To do that, we need to follow Paul and Julie as they carried out the plan Mr. Woods worked out with them.

First, it's important to understand that by the time they went to Mr. Woods they were deeply in debt and had elected to file for a Chapter 13 reorganization under the Federal Bankruptcy Code. Appendices E, F, and G of this book contain a summary of Chapters 7, 12, and 13 of the Federal Bankruptcy Code. The summary is adapted from *Bankruptcy: Do It Yourself* and *Chapter 13: The Federal Plan to Repay Your Debts,* both by Janet Kosel (Nolo Press, 1987).

Table 10.1 is a summary of Paul and Julie's financial condition when Mr. Woods first saw them. The figures on the left reflect what an average family in their salary range would normally spend in a month on various household expenses. The figures on the right reflect what Paul and Julie had budgeted.

As you can see, Paul and Julie had a financial problem that could be solved only by creating more income or by spending less. Since more income wasn't an option for them, they had to spend less.

In reality, less spending is the answer for the vast majority of debt problems. Given the chance, most of us would be able to spend almost unlimited amounts of money, so more money coming in usually means more money going out. Remember that Paul had already tried a bill-consolidation loan through his company's credit union. Usually that helps for a short while because the monthly payments are reduced through a lower interest, longer-term loan. But unless the conditions that caused the initial problems are changed, the end result will be even more debt. In Paul's case, he had to pay back not only the bill-consolidation loan but also the credit card bills he had accumulated a few months later, so he was actually worse off than he was before he got the bill-consolidation loan.

Table 10.1
Paul and Julie Averal's "As Is" Budget
Compared to a Recommended Spending Plan
for a Family with a Monthly Income of $1,800 Net

Average Spending		The Averal's "As Is" Budget	
Taxes	(taken out)	Taxes	(taken out)
Charities	$180	Charities	$ 0
Housing	567	Housing	1,240
Auto	230	Auto	280
Food	240	Food	200
Clothing	80	Clothing	0
Medical	80	Medical	0
Insurance	70	Insurance	0
Ent. & Recreation	95	Ent. & Recreation	25
Debt	80	Debt	250
Miscellaneous	90	Miscellaneous	25
Savings	80	Savings	0
Total	$1,792	Total	$2,020

A glance at the Averal's "As Is" Budget tells much of the story. Their budget could have handled the spending of 30 to 35 percent of their net pay for housing (about $540-$630 per month), but they had committed themselves to payments that were nearly 60 percent of their income, or $1,080 per month. When utilities were added, their expenses for housing came to more than $1,240. They could not make it on such a budget, even from the beginning. They were running a deficit from the time they made the first mortgage payment until the home was sold.

Note also that they were overcommitted in the categories of transportation (cars) and outstanding debt. Those debts were the obvious result of the lack of money created each month by the high house payment. When necessities came up, such as clothes, insurance, or car repairs, Paul used credit to make up the difference. The overcommitment he made regarding the cars reflected a weakness in Paul toward cars. His weakness in this area is not unusual. In fact it is quite common in most young men. During the dating years in high school and college, they place such great importance on their automobiles that they become personal status symbols. That is a poor attitude when Mom and Dad are paying the bills and the young person is still single, but it is a disaster when the young man gets married and continues to cling to the same values.

When you look at the budget for clothing, entertainment, and medical/dental expenses, you will note that Paul and Julie allocated nothing on a regular monthly basis for those items. That does not mean they found a miraculous way to keep their clothes from wearing out or their teeth from developing cavities. It means they did not have money for those items and so left them out of their budget. When these expenses came due, as they were bound to, Paul and Julie had to rely on credit cards to make up the deficit. That is why so many couples say they use their credit cards only for necessities. Often that's true, except that other spending creates the need to use the cards for the necessities.

Mr. Woods gave Paul and Julie some suggestions to help them resolve both their immediate and their long-term problems.

1. Use the funds they already had on hand to pay the VISA bill and the outstanding balance on the car Paul had returned. Mr. Woods made direct contact with the owner of the car lot and told him what had happened with Paul. The owner agreed to accept a reduced amount in total payment of the bill, which saved Paul $300.

2. Each month continue to meet the obligations established by the bankruptcy court. With Paul and Julie's combined incomes, they were able to pay at least the minimum amounts due.

3. Make a budget showing what they could afford to pay for housing, assuming that their bankruptcy debts were paid and they had only Paul's income. This showed how totally out of line their housing expenses were with their income. They decided to sell the home and find housing that would meet their needs.

4. Assign Julie the task of managing the books in their home. She would pay the bills each month, and she and Paul would review the budget together at least once a month.

5. Make a budget that they could live with, once the bankruptcy payments were completed, and assume in that budget that they would have only Paul's income to work with and that they would be repaying, in total, everyone to whom they owed money.

The budget shown in Table 10.2 is the Averals' "Want To" Budget. It shows where Paul and Julie wanted to be when the bankruptcy was cleared. Note the reduced amount for housing, which is a much more realistic figure for Paul's income. The new spending plan meant that Paul and Julie had to give up their home and rent for a period of time, but that was a small sacrifice compared to the peace they had lost when they committed themselves to buying that home.

Table 10.2
"Want to" Budget for Paul and Julie Averal
Based on an After-Tax Income of $1,400 Per Month

Taxes	(Taken out)
Charities	$150
Housing	450
Auto	200
Food	250
Clothing	50
Medical	50
Insurance	50
Ent. & Rec.	100
Debt	0
Miscellaneous	50
Savings	50
Total	$1,400

Paul and Julie had some questions about their situation that are common to couples in their situation. I thought it might be helpful to others to review those questions.

What effect will the Chapter 13 bankruptcy have on our future credit?

According to the Fair Credit Reporting Act, any credit reporting agency can report that you filed for bankruptcy protection for up to ten years after the date of that action. Therefore, any potential lender inquiring about your credit history will receive that report.

Is there any way to clear our credit rating?

Not really. Too often in our society people act as if there are no consequences of a bankruptcy, but that is simply not true. The bankruptcy laws were originally created to help balance an unjust system that sent poor people to prison for bad debts. But too often today they are abused by people who don't want to repay money they have already spent. Consequently, legitimate creditors look upon those who use bankruptcy as deadbeats who don't want to pay their bills. The net effect is that those who go bankrupt are often refused credit from legitimate lenders later.

Is there any way we can prove that we are honest and reestablish a good credit rating?

Yes. Once the bankruptcy is cleared, you can continue to pay the entirety of the debts you owe. After a creditor is completely paid off, ask him to write you a letter of recommendation and send a copy to his local credit reporting agencies. Many agencies will include letters of recommendation in their official credit reports. But you can also give the letters to a potential lender when you apply for a loan yourself.

The best recommendation I can give to anyone is this: pay back what you borrow and never borrow frivolously. (A summary of the Fair Credit Reporting Act is given in Appendix B of this book.)

What would happen if Paul's union went on strike or if he lost his job for any reason?

You should notify the bankruptcy court trustee immediately. Usually they will work out a temporary moratorium with your creditors. However, if the situation lasts for any extended period of time, the bankruptcy judge may elect to dissolve your debts through a Chapter 7 dissolution. In other words, your assets are sold and the creditors paid with the proceeds of the sale.

Anyone who is not under a court order, such as a bankruptcy, needs to stay in direct contact with his creditors and tell them the absolute truth. Most creditors will work with a debtor who has temporary financial problems, as long as he is trying to be fair and honest.

11
Don't Use Borrowed Money for Speculative Ventures

Many men can identify with Ron Hawkins. He was a good person who tried to better himself and his family. Because he came from a relatively poor background—too little money and too many children—he was pretty much left to fend for himself. When he finished high school, he thought about going to college but he wasn't a scholarship candidate, and his parents had no money to help him. So he went into the Air Force for two years on reserve status. He saved as much money as he could and then started at a junior college in his hometown. He lived on his own, as there wasn't room in his parents' home.

While he was in college, he worked nearly full time in the evenings and on weekends. He wasn't a straight-A student, but he made fairly good grades. He was sure he could have done even better if he had had more time to study.

He and Sue met when he was at the state university completing his last two years of college. They were married during Ron's last year in school and actually lived better than Ron had by himself. Sue had a nice off-campus condominium her parents had bought when she went to college.

Sue's father was a very successful trial attorney. Her parents were committed churchgoers. The church Sue had attended most of her life was socially "correct" and, as she put it, "Most of the sermons were straight out of *The Wall Street Journal* or *U.S. News and World Report.*"

Sue's parents didn't consciously indulge her. They simply included her in an indulgent lifestyle that meant a new wardrobe each year, a new car every other year, and winter vacations in Colorado.

She knew other people didn't have as much as her parents; she had several close friends who came from middle income families. But she also experienced strife in her own family because her mother and father fought constantly. Usually their arguments revolved around her father's commitment to his work and the fact that he was rarely around. In truth, many times Sue, her mother, and one of Sue's friends spent those holiday trips to Aspen or Vail without Sue's father. He rarely accompanied them. By the time Sue was a senior in high school, her parents were separated. The separation later became semi-permanent, although there was never a divorce.

In college Sue met Ron. She fell in love with him and married him within the year. As is so often the case, although Sue was not the least bit embarrassed by Ron's humble background, Ron was. Visiting Sue's home was agony for Ron because it made him feel inadequate. Nothing Sue could say would convince Ron that all was not bliss in that beautiful home. His goal was set: eventually he would have the same kind of home.

I share this background to help you realize that when someone gets into debt from indulgence and greed, it is often not the result of a conscious decision. It is the result of decisions clouded by good intentions and rationalizations. I believe the worst thing that can happen to anyone is to achieve his financial goals. Then he is able to surround himself with enough "things" to avoid facing the reality of how miserable he really is. If you don't believe that's true, look at the amount of alcohol and drugs consumed by the "up and outers."

After college, Ron took a job with a major stock brokerage firm. He had a good aptitude and personality, and he did quite well. But within a few years Sue feared she was seeing the same attitudes developing in Ron that she had seen in her father. Ron was consumed by business and had a drive to succeed that pushed everything and everyone else into the background.

Sue began to nag Ron about his lack of care for his family and his lack of involvement in their lives. In reality, he spent about the same amount of time with his family that many young businessmen do—very little.

The more Sue nagged, the less Ron knew how to handle it, so he began to substitute time at the office for time with her. As his income grew, so did opportunities to take part in some of the investments his company brokered. He began to risk larger amounts of borrowed money, secured only by his signature. Sue didn't know about most of the loans, because the lenders for most of them did not require her signature. As with many fast-moving investment markets (this one was in commercial properties), the lenders were only too willing to lend large amounts of money with little or no collateral and secured only by the signatures of the principal parties involved.

Within a few years Ron's net worth had grown to more than $200,000 and, with it, grew his ability to borrow even more. He bought a new home in a wealthy neighborhood, in spite of Sue's objections.

Ron even made several attempts to spend more time at home, but each time another deal would develop and he would spend weeks of sixteen-hour days putting it together. When she saw the volumes of forms that had to be filed with their tax statements each year, Sue asked Ron to sit down and discuss their finances. Ron said he would but never took the time to do so. He knew that Sue wouldn't agree with much of what he was doing, so it was just easier to avoid telling her.

As time passed, Sue felt more and more excluded from what had become the focus of Ron's activities. All she knew about their finances was how much Ron gave her to run the household. He was extremely generous, and Sue usually got whatever she asked for.

Then suddenly the economy, which had been inflating the real estate ventures Ron was handling, cooled off. Interest rates rose precipitously and, with the interest rate increases, the real estate market that had grown as a result of borrowed money suddenly stopped cold.

Within one month, what had been a hot market cooled to the point where no banker was willing to lend any money on speculative ventures. In fact, bankers began to call some of the demand notes that had been issued to numerous investors, including Ron.

Almost overnight, Ron found himself with virtually no income, for land sales had all but stopped, and the banks were unwilling to extend the signature notes secured by his land investments.

When Ron couldn't sell any of the properties the banks were holding as collateral on his notes, the bankers suggested that he assign an interest in his home as substitute collateral. To do this he needed Sue's agreement, since the home was in both their names. Ron approached Sue that evening after their kids had gone to bed. "Sue, I've got a problem and I need your help," Ron said timidly.

Sue felt her heart take a flip as her mind conjured up the worst circumstances imaginable. She had inwardly assumed that Ron might be seeing someone else, just as her father had done. Now she feared that he, too, wanted a separation—or worse.

"What kind of a problem, Ron?" she asked defiantly.

"Without a second mortgage on the house, the banks won't renew some of the notes I have on the land investments I've made." Inwardly Sue breathed a sigh of relief, but outwardly the tough shell she had assumed as a defense stayed intact as she answered in a biting tone, "And just how much do you owe on your great investments, Ron?"

Ron winced at her tone and at the emphasis she had placed on the words "your" and "Ron." "I don't know exactly," he lied.

"Well give me an approximate figure. Or do you think I'm too dumb to be trusted with information like that?" Sue asked with tears coming to her eyes in spite of herself.

"Honey, you know I don't think you're dumb," Ron said with his head down.

"Well, you must. You have never once told me what you're doing. I learn more at the Christmas party when your so-called partners are there than I do living in the same house with you."

Ron didn't know where to go with the conversation. They had often been at this point before. He had wanted to tell Sue what he was doing and why, but when she took such an offensive position he just backed off and buried himself in his work. But he couldn't do that now. If he didn't assign the collateral, the banks would call his notes immediately and he would lose everything. Worse than that, he would probably still owe several thousands of dollars after the properties were sold in this down market. He knew if he could hold on and ride out the bad times the land values would recover. But the house was the only thing of value he had to pledge.

"Listen, honey, I know you've been hurt by my actions in the past, but this is a real crisis. If I can't give the banks some additional collateral, they will call the notes on the properties and sell them at cut-rate prices," Ron said as honestly as he could.

"You still didn't answer my question, Ron. How much do you owe?"

As he started to speak, Ron flinched at what he knew would be a verbal assault from Sue. "I owe nearly $200,000," he said.

And to his utter amazement he heard Sue reply, "Well good, then we'll be totally broke when this thing is over, I suspect. I'll be glad to see it all gone."

"Why did you say that?" Ron asked in total puzzlement.

"Because I have prayed for a long time that something would happen to bring all this to a head. We aren't married; we're just two people living in the same house, sharing the same bed.

"You really don't understand, do you?" she continued, as Ron dropped his head again. "I don't care about the money, the house, or anything money can buy. I would be perfectly satisfied in a subdivision home with a husband who came home at five and spent time with his family. Ron, I panic when I think about the years after our kids leave and I'm left here by myself. My mother started drinking because she couldn't stand it. I don't know what I would do."

Because of the emotional state he was in, Ron didn't hear what Sue was really trying to say. All he heard was his wife saying she wished she had married someone else. In an attitude of resignation he asked, "Will you sign the power of attorney on the house, Sue?"

"You didn't hear a word I said, did you?" she spit out. "Yes, I'll sign so you can get your loans renewed. I don't want to hurt you; I just want us to be one—and we're not. But I can tell you this. When the bottom falls out of your business, your so-called friends are going to leave you high and dry. Then what are you going to do—turn and run too?"

"I have never run from anything in my life," Ron responded. "I believe the investments I have made are sound, and I'll stand by the people who have invested with me, no matter what."

"You may get a chance to find out what 'no matter what' is," Sue said. "I can remember my dad talking about clients suing their financial advisers during a bad time in the real estate market. Yours will, too."

"The people who invest with me know that I always try to do what's best for them," Ron said defensively. "I can't help what the government does about interest rates. They know that."

"Get into the real world, Ron," she said. "Those people won't care if you spend twenty hours a day working for them. What most of them care about is that you sold them an investment that lost money."

Ron pledged his home as collateral against the bank loans and was able to hold off the foreclosures for the time being. But several months passed, and the economic situation didn't get any better. In fact, it got considerably worse. Many of the biggest banks had hundreds of nonperforming loans and began to experience financial problems themselves. Loan managers were fired or moved, and new management was brought in to deal with the crisis. All real estate loans that had not been paid on in more than three months were immediately called as due and payable—Ron's included.

It didn't matter what arrangements had been made in the past. The rule was, pay up in full or surrender the properties. In an effort to salvage some of the more valuable properties, Ron approached some of his wealthiest clients, who stood to lose the most if the ventures failed. He asked them to put up the necessary capital to collateralize the notes on the land they were already invested in. In exchange, he would subordinate his position (take a lesser profit after they got their money when the land was sold). He also guaranteed their additional collateral with a third mortgage on his home—without telling Sue.

Unfortunately, the interest rates remained high, and the real estate market dropped even further as desperate bankers dumped large inventories of unsold land on the already depressed market. Land prices dropped more than 70 percent from the pre-recession high. Now haggard bankers called for additional collateral on any outstanding notes. The investors Ron had convinced to put up additional collateral were faced with either risking more of their assets or losing what they had already pledged. They opted to lose what they had pledged and sue Ron and his partners for negligence.

Faced with the collapsed real estate market and a pending lawsuit, Ron's three partners elected to file for personal bankruptcy protection. It was only then that Ron learned that all of their personal assets were held in their wives' names and that, other than the now defunct properties, they had no assets to lose. The investors were left with nothing to attach except Ron.

Ron knew he had done nothing illegal or unethical in his dealings with his investors, and he was certain he would be vindicated if the case came to trial. He tried to settle with the disgruntled investors but, since they already had a third mortgage on his home, they decided to sue out of anger and vindictiveness over the losses they had suffered.

Ultimately, the case came to trial and Ron waived his right to a trial by jury so the case would be heard and decided by a single judge. Because of a lack of funds, Ron had elected to use an inexperienced attorney who had little courtroom experience. The investors, on the other hand, used a highly qualified trial attorney. He depicted Ron as a scheming manipulator who talked the investors into risking money in ventures they could not possibly understand. The conclusion the judge reached: guilty as charged.

The decision broke Ron. Not only was he judged to be guilty of defrauding investors, but his license to sell securities was suspended for five years. He was penniless and without the means to earn a living.

12

Commit to Faithfully Repay Creditors

Nearly a month had passed since the trial in which Ron had been found guilty. Since he lacked any unattached assets, the judge had awarded the plaintiffs a summary judgment that allowed them to attach anything of value Ron owned now or in the future. The plaintiffs elected to force Ron into bankruptcy by notifying all of Ron's outstanding creditors that they intended to attach and sell any and all properties Ron owned, including his home. With that action imminent, several of the unsecured creditors filed suit for judgment. Ron's family problems also continued to grow.

"Ron, you told me this lawsuit would amount to nothing, and now I see we have a judgment against us," Sue said, shaking the paper that the sheriff had delivered that day. "Do you call this nothing?"

"I'm really sorry, Sue. I wanted to tell you, but I just didn't know how. The judge decided against us. We lost. But that's not the worst of it. Now the investors have decided to use the judgment to force a bankruptcy. They know that if they demand payment, I won't be able to pay. So they're demanding a forced sale of the house and everything else. Then the other creditors will be forced to do the same. We'll be wiped out. I wouldn't blame you if you decided to leave too.

Because I lost the lawsuit, the SEC is suspending my license for five years. I won't even have a way to earn a living."

"Ron, I don't care about this house or the investments. I told you that before. I just want to be a part of your life. I will stick by you because we promised God that our marriage is for better or worse. I love you, and we'll be able to see this thing through together," Sue said in a softening tone. The tears welled up in her eyes. "I know I haven't been a good wife. I thought you were going down the same path I saw my own father go down before he left my mother, and it frightened me."

"I'm really sorry, Sue," Ron said as he put his arms around her. "I didn't know that's what you were thinking. I thought I was doing all these deals for you and the kids. Now I realize that I was doing them to feed my own ego and insecurity. I feared being poor so much I was willing to throw away the most important assets God ever gave me. Maybe in the long run this disaster will be the best thing that ever happened to us."

Ron felt a burden lift from his shoulders. "You know, it's funny. We're totally broke and facing bankruptcy, but I finally feel free. Maybe you have to hit bottom before you can begin to look up."

"Ron, I feel that we should use this opportunity. Why don't you go to each of the creditors and ask them not to force you into bankruptcy? Tell them that we intend to pay every dime of the money back if they will work with us."

"But how in the world will we ever do that?" Ron asked, looking at his wife with an air of appreciation. "We're dead broke, and I lost my license."

"Then there's no way to go but up, is there?" Sue asked.

"That's for sure," Ron replied. "You know, Sue, it may sound crazy but I am actually excited. I'm just going to talk to the creditors and tell them the truth—that if they join in the bankruptcy they won't get anything because the first and second mortgages will wipe out any money from the house and the cars are leased. But, if they will trust us, they'll get paid. I'm going to start calling first thing tomorrow."

Ron went to each of the creditors, most of whom were banks holding deficiency agreements on the property loans, and asked them not to force him into bankruptcy. When he was asked how he would ever repay the money he owed, he responded, "I don't know, but if you don't join in the bankruptcy action, I promise I'll repay every dime I owe you. In the meantime, I'll get a job and pay you what I can each month."

Ron's biggest creditor was the largest bank in town. Based on the current value of the land they had foreclosed, the bank estimated Ron owed them over $200,000. Ron met with the bank president (a former client) and asked him not to join in the bankruptcy action.

"But Ron, I have a responsibility to our stockholders," was the banker's reply. "If you're hiding any assets and we don't join the lawsuit, I could be sued for negligence."

"Sir, I give you my word that what you see on the paper before you is everything I own in the world, and it isn't much," Ron said.

"But why don't you want me to join in the lawsuit, Ron? If this is all you own and our agreement is thrown into the bankruptcy too, you won't have to repay us either."

"Because I know I got myself in this mess and I want to do what I think is the honorable thing," Ron replied with confidence. "That's why I'm asking my creditors to trust me. Those who join in the bankruptcy action have voluntarily changed the agreement, and it's no longer my responsibility to fulfill the original obligation."

"Well, Ron, that's about the strangest proposal I've ever heard in my years as a banker, but I'll take this to my board of directors at our meeting this Thursday. I'll recommend we go along with you on this, but the final decision is up to the board."

"I understand, sir, and I sincerely appreciate your confidence in me," Ron said as he started to leave.

"Ron, I believe you're an honest man, and you always did a good job for me. You made errors in judgment on some of the land deals we funded, but who hasn't? You borrowed too much on speculation, but we loaned too much on the same projects. It could just as well have been me the investors of this bank sued, except that we have more money to ride out the downturn."

"Thank you, sir. That really does encourage me. I trust we'll both see some miracles."

Later that week Ron heard from the banker that the board had agreed to maintain their notes and not join the bankruptcy.

The bankruptcy proceeded rapidly, with all but three creditors joining in the proceeding. Ron and Sue did not contest the bankruptcy action and surrendered all of their personal assets voluntarily, including personal jewelry—even Sue's wedding rings. The bankruptcy judge instructed them that they had the right to maintain ownership of certain personal assets, such as the wedding rings, but they refused, saying they wanted the creditors to receive as much as possible.

Ultimately, the disgruntled investors who had brought the action received nothing for their trouble except bills from their attorneys.

In the meantime, Ron had been searching for a job that would allow him to provide for his family. He decided eventually that selling was the only thing he knew how to do, and he took a job on a commission basis in product sales with a national company. Within three months he had met the minimum quota set by the company and was earning an average annual income of about $30,000. He and Sue worked out a budget that would allow them to live on an income of $24,000 a year, with the rest going to pay the creditors they still owed from the land deals. In the case of the large bank, Ron and Sue were able to pay an average of $200 a month. Although the interest alone on their debt would have been over $1,500 a month, the bank president elected to forgo the interest charges so that they would not be losing ground each month.

Ron and Sue settled into a greatly modified lifestyle and committed themselves to getting to know each other better and discovering what the future had in store for them.

13

Two Common Errors That Lead to Debt

Ron had violated two fundamental principles that ultimately resulted in his financial disaster. The first was allowing a get-rich-quick mentality to control his decisions.

ALLOWING A GET-RICH-QUICK MENTALITY TO GOVERN DECISIONS

Symptoms of get-rich-quick are evident in many of the investment schemes in this country and around the world today. There are three distinguishing characteristics.

RISKING BORROWED MONEY

If investments in get-rich-quick schemes were limited to available cash only, most people would be wary of losing it. But somehow it is easier to risk borrowed money because it seems almost free —at least until you have to pay it back. The same principle applies to buying consumer goods on credit. Credit card companies understand the mentality of leveraged purchases (purchases bought with borrowed money). People who use their credit cards for clothes, food, and vacations are prime candidates for overbuying. Credit card issuers can prove to a merchant statistically that those people will buy more and pay a higher price than those who buy only with cash.

There is no argument that through the use of leveraged (borrowed) money you can get rich a lot faster. But there is as well no argument that the majority of those who do so end up losing it all in the long run, for the mentality that prompted them to take the initial risk will prompt them to take ever bigger risks; eventually they will get wiped out in a bad economy. You don't have to look any further than the oil industry in America to verify that principle. Thousands of multi-millionaires were totally wiped out between 1983 and 1985, when the price of oil dropped precipitously. But it wasn't the price of oil that destroyed them; it was the fact that they had borrowed against everything they owned to expand their investments. When the bottom fell out of the market, as it always does eventually, they lost everything.

The same principle destroyed much of the fortune accumulated by a well-known oil tycoon. Two of his sons decided to corner the silver market and nearly succeeded in doing so. But when the price of silver began to fall, they were unable to cover the margin accounts they held in connection with the trading they did in silver. They had purchased silver contracts on credit but were forced to sell those contracts at drastically reduced prices. Then they were forced to sell other assets to repay the money borrowed on the silver contracts. Before the cycle ended, the majority of a multi-billion-dollar estate had evaporated.

GETTING INVOLVED IN THINGS YOU DON'T UNDERSTAND

The second element of the get-rich-quick mentality—taking financial risks in fields you know little or nothing about—is dangerous if there is any possibility of losing sizable amounts of money in the investment. It would be difficult to convince a chemist to invest large amounts of borrowed money in a scheme to turn lead into gold. A chemist understands the physics of the elements too well to be trapped by such a wild scheme (usually!). So the logical candidate for such a venture is a businessman who made his fortune in frozen pizzas. He knows pizzas well, but knows nothing at all about the molecular structure of lead and gold. Obviously you won't find every pizza baron investing in lead-to-gold conversion schemes, but you definitely won't find any chemists doing it.

Several years ago a scheme came through Atlanta that was a classic example of the type of investment I'm talking about. I found out about it because I'm frequently called on to evaluate new get-rich-quick schemes, and some of the potential investors wanted my appraisal of the project. The scheme involved a revolutionary automobile engine that supposedly ran on a gas plasma. The engine was small and lightweight and could fit into a Volkswagen-sized car. It was claimed that the engine could generate over 200 horsepower (the equivalent of a large V-8 engine).

But best of all, it ran on water—ordinary faucet water. All you needed for a fuel supply was a jug of water. When you needed a refill, you simply poured the water into the tank. Now let me ask you, who would not invest in this revolutionary idea? Automotive engineers and physicists? They just laughed at the idea.

I tried to get a look at one of the engines that supposedly was powering the Volkswagen and scheduled several appointments. But each time, an emergency arose that kept the "inventor" from being able to show me the engine. Usually the emergency was related to "hit squads" the inventor claimed the automotive companies had hired to kill him and steal his invention.

Before the plasma engine scheme was shut down, several people had invested tens of thousands of dollars, much of it borrowed, in return for shares in a company that supposedly was going to be bigger than General Motors. As you can guess, those investors are still waiting for their fortunes. And they are still paying off their loans. It's interesting to note that some of those investors still insist that the idea is real and that the car companies are keeping it off the market. They have convinced themselves that the inventor is in hiding, which is why he disappeared so suddenly and why they have not heard anything from him.

The lesson to be learned is this: Stay with what you know best and you'll lose a lot less money in the long run. Ron was particularly good at evaluating and selling registered securities, and he made a very good living doing that. It was when he ventured into land development that he got in over his head.

MAKING HASTY DECISIONS

Ron's decision to borrow excessive amounts of money for his investment projects was compounded by the fact that when things started to go sour he rushed into more borrowing and talked other investors into doing the same thing. Had he counseled them (and himself) to stop and really think about their decisions before acting, the judge probably would have ruled in his favor. One of the key elements of the prosecution's case was the fact that, as an investment adviser, Ron had the opportunity to put undue pressure on his clients to act hastily.

In the final analysis, it was the charged nature of the adviser-investor relationship and the inherent conflict between Ron's interests and the interests of his clients that caused the judge to be so harsh with him. The judge's point was well taken. He wanted to make an example of Ron so that others in the position of trusted adviser would not take that responsibility lightly again.

I said that Ron had violated two basic principles in his finances. The first was having a get-rich-quick attitude. The second was ignoring his primary adviser: his wife, Sue.

IGNORING THE PRIMARY ADVISER

I don't think I can stress this principle too strongly. It is very dangerous for a husband or wife to ignore the primary adviser: the spouse. When you live with someone in a relationship as close as husband and wife, there are bound to be problems. Since opposites tend to attract, you probably won't agree about everything. In fact, you may never totally agree about anything. But that's okay, as long as you know how to work it out together and reach a reasonable compromise.

Ron's background made him a candidate for excesses in the area of finances. Often it is not the person from a wealthy background who is obsessed by success but rather the one from a modest or poor background. We all have the tendency to overcompensate for what we lacked as children.

I came out of a relatively poor background in a wealthy community and I tend to store rather than spend. Fortunately, my wife prefers to sit on furniture and grow flowers, or probably I would be sitting on orange crates and investing in antique cars. She helps to balance my extremes, as I balance hers.

These distinctives in personality types should not be ignored when a couple works out the decision-making function in their marriage. We have stereotyped the roles of husband and wife. When we do that we fail to recognize psychological realities.

When a husband avoids or ignores his wife's counsel on any matter, including finances, he should expect his goals to be hindered. The same can be said for a wife who does not give her husband respect as the head of his family.

Thus the stereotype does not work when it diminishes the balance built into a marriage. Even when the husband is the dominant personality and the decision-maker, there is still the danger that he will exclude his wife from financial decisions, investments, and major purchases, such as cars or boats.

But the stereotype completely breaks down when the husband is not naturally a dominant person. Sometimes he is, but in a high percentage of the families I have counseled, the wife is the dominant personality and the decision-maker. In these cases the wife must learn to listen to the counsel of her husband, just as dominant husbands must listen to their less dominant wives. If the wife hasn't learned to do this, she will be seen as pushy, domineering, or unsubmissive.

Husbands and wives are supposed to function as a single working unit, each with different but essential abilities. Certainly those abilities will overlap in many areas, and often that will lead to differences of opinions. But just as certainly, without the balance that each can bring to the marriage, great errors in judgment will be made.

It has been my observation that a dominant woman operating on her own initiative will accumulate debt through credit cards and store accounts, because she buys too many clothes or too much furniture. A dominant husband operating on his own initiative will accumulate debt through the purchase of boats, airplanes, and other investments. Men don't buy very often, but when they do, they buy big.

FACING A CHAPTER 7 BANKRUPTCY WITH PRUDENCE AND HONOR

Though the consequences of a Chapter 7 bankruptcy are very severe, a bankrupcy may indeed occur when a get-rich-quick scheme fails.

Ron and Sue experienced the total dissolution of their assets through a creditor-initiated bankruptcy action. In most instances, such action by any three creditors is sufficient to force a bankruptcy. In Ron's case, he elected to file bankruptcy rather than to allow the few demanding creditors to sell off his remaining assets to their benefit and to the detriment of all the others.

A bankruptcy action will usually provide only a fraction of the total debt owed to creditors, but creditors are required to accept the liquidation proceeds as total settlement of their debt. Again, in Ron's case, he and Sue committed themselves to repaying everyone who agreed not to join the bankruptcy action. They felt that those creditors who elected to take the bankruptcy proceeds did so voluntarily and thus settled the debt. To be as fair as possible to the creditors who joined the bankruptcy, Ron and Sue retained no salable assets, even though bankruptcy action allows the debtor to keep a small amount of the home equity (if there is a home), one automobile, and a limited amount of cash. Unlike many others who file bankruptcy for their convenience, Ron placed all assets held in Sue's name into the asset pool as well. They withheld nothing from the creditors.

Bankruptcy is never an action to be taken lightly. The financial consequences and the damage to a reputation are long-lasting. A creditor has a right to expect to recover the money he has loaned in good faith. I believe that Ron and Sue fulfilled this principle by going to each of the creditors and explaining why they decided to file for bankruptcy. They believed that the disgruntled investors would force them to sell off all their assets and that the unsecured creditors had a right to a share, if they so elected. However, when Ron and Sue approached the creditors, they also explained their total financial situation and indicated that the sale of all their assets would yield only a small fraction of the total debt. They then asked each creditor not to join the bankruptcy action on the promise (in writing) that they would repay all debts in total at a future date, if they obtained the funds.

This action was taken against the counsel of their attorney, who recommended that they place all debts in the bankruptcy and clear them. He said they could choose to repay the deficiencies later, if and when they had the funds. Ron and Sue decided not to take his advice because they thought it should be the choice of the creditor to take what was available immediately or trust them to repay later.

Because of the loan defaults as a result of the bankruptcy, Ron also owed nearly $100,000 in taxes to the IRS. Under a rule called Forgiveness of Debt, most of the unrecovered loan balances were declared income and as such were subject to taxes, interest, and penalties. The IRS agreed to waive the penalties, but Ron (and Sue) still ended up owing nearly $100,000 in back taxes. Since a bankruptcy action cannot remove tax-related debt, those taxes still remained. But without the ability to pay even a small fraction of the debt, and without assets, Ron could do nothing but allow the debt to continue accumulating interest.

A short while later they received another financial shock through a letter from the IRS agent assigned to their case. He noted that since they had sold their home, the gain on that sale would also be taxable if they did not purchase a home of equal or greater value within the next two years. "Just a note to remind you," he wrote. Needless to say, Ron and Sue felt like the weight of the world had been dropped on them again.

"We're going to make a budget that will help us control our spending and manage the surpluses we have," Ron announced at the dinner table that evening. The children groaned. "Oh great, Dad. We just got a reprieve from voluntary poverty, and now you make it voluntary."

"Not so," Ron said cheerfully. "We're going to all work together to manage our expenses so we won't squander what God has given us. Then He'll know we can manage more later."

Soon the children were excited about planning what to do with a surplus. First Ron and Sue explained about the debts that were still outstanding, especially the ones to the bank. "They had the most to lose," Ron told the children, "so they showed the most faith in us. We need to pay them back before we assume any of the money is ours to manage."

Ron also explained about the IRS debt and that it would need to be paid, to which the kids booed and hissed. They had seen and heard the callous way the agent assigned to their case had acted when he thought they were trying to hide some assets.

"Guys, you need to remember that the government didn't cause our problems. I did. We might object to paying the taxes because it is a lot of money, but we need to remember that it's a consequence of my actions, not theirs. If I had not borrowed and taken risks, we wouldn't have a tax problem. It was greed that caused our problems, not the government."

Ron and Sue planned a budget based on Ron's present income and decided that they would be able to manage quite well when they didn't have the debt burden to pay each month.

Two years passed as Ron and Sue continued to pay a few hundred dollars a year on debts that accumulated thousands of dollars in interest each year. Ron did well in selling real estate, and his income increased to nearly $35,000 a year. They increased the shares they paid to the bank, and to the IRS. Two of their children had been in a fairly expensive private school prior to the financial problems. Ron and Sue decided that the money for the school should be paid to creditors, so they decided to remove the kids from the private school and send them to a public school. Sue later said that Ron had more difficulty with that decision than with any other. It's one thing to take responsibility for your mistakes, and quite another to ask your children to suffer for them. It was the only school they had ever attended, and all their friends were there.

When Sue told the principal, he was shocked.

"You can't do that, Sue," he said. "Your children have been here since the school started. You're a part of this family."

"We have made up our minds, John," Sue replied. "We don't believe it is our right to keep our children in a private school when we owe so much. Other people's children go to public schools and survive. Our decision is made."

"How do the children feel about this?" the principal asked.

"Naturally, they're disappointed," Sue answered. "But they understand what we must do and why."

They agreed that the children would remain in the school until the spring break, which was about two weeks away. In the meantime, Sue went to the local public schools and made the necessary arrangements to have the children's records transferred. Later that week Sue received a call from the principal of the private school.

"Sue, I wanted to let you know that we had a meeting of the school board last night and that they voted to provide scholarships for your children."

"That's wonderful news, John! The children will be thrilled to hear it. Please tell the members of the committee how much we appreciate it and that we will repay the funds when we can."

"No, Sue," the principal replied. "I told them that you and Ron would take it as an obligation to repay. This is a gift from us to you. Several members of the board have already paid the tuition and book money themselves."

That evening Ron and Sue told their children the good news.

"Kids, I think this is God's way of saying thank you for your obedience to what we asked you to do," Ron said with tears in his eyes. The older two children clapped and yelled about what they viewed as a miracle on their behalf.

A few months later Ron was in his office when he got a call from the president of the bank.

"Ron, could we have lunch tomorrow? I'd like to talk to you about your outstanding loans."

"Certainly," Ron replied, feeling that old queasy feeling in the pit of his stomach. He imagined all kinds of things. Perhaps the bank had decided to sue him for collection. But that didn't make any sense. He still didn't have any assets to sell. They were living in a rented house and driving a six-year-old car. And they had been making regular monthly payments, even if they were pitifully small.

The next day at lunch Mr. Cross, the bank president, said, "Ron, I want to thank you for living up to my confidence in you. I have to tell you that I had a dickens of a time convincing the other members of the board to go along with your plan. Some thought you were pulling a fast one on us; others thought it would be better to get the whole thing over with and write off the bad debts. But your commitment and dependability to make a payment each month has been the subject of praise at nearly every board meeting for the last two years."

"Thank you, Mr. Cross. But I don't think I deserve any praise for doing what is my responsibility anyway," Ron replied honestly.

"Perhaps not, Ron, but I'll tell you this: not one other major debtor to the bank has repaid any of the bad syndication loans. Most of them went bankrupt and put all their assets in someone else's name. Doing what is right is not the norm today.

"We recently had a contact on the land you surrendered on your loans. Two days ago we sold the land, thus clearing your notes totally."

"That's great, Mr. Cross. I know you didn't have to do that, and I sincerely appreciate it."

"But that's not all, Ron," he continued. "Our board has agreed to do something that I have never heard of a bank doing before. They have agreed to return all of the proceeds above the actual loan amounts to you. I have a check in the amount of $380,000 made out to you."

Ron was utterly speechless.

"Mr. Cross, I really don't know what to say except that this truly is the last thing I expected."

"That makes two of us, Ron. Banks and bankers normally aren't very benevolent toward delinquent debtors, but we all recognize something different in your life. Thank you for being honest and meeting the commitments you made. I can tell you that is truly unusual in people facing financial difficulties."

Ron could hardly wait to get home and tell Sue the great news. When he burst through the door she met him saying, "I already know, honey."

"How in the world could you know about it?" Ron asked. "I just found out an hour ago."

"News like this travels faster than AT&T," Sue replied. "I have had two calls already this morning. One from a friend of a friend at the bank, and the second from one of your ex-partners."

"Which one?" Ron asked cautiously.

"Bob," Sue replied with a hint of irritation in her voice. "He said he had heard that one of the partnership's investments had sold and wondered what his share would be. He asked that you call him when you came in. Are you planning to divide the proceeds with them, Ron?"

"Absolutely not!" Ron said emphatically. "They weren't willing to share in the losses, so they don't have any right to the profits. We'll pay off the IRS debt and decide where to put the rest of it."

"Remember our plan, Ron," Sue said jestingly, "to be debt-free. Does that mean owning a home? "

"Absolutely," Ron replied. "If I calculate properly, we should be able to pay the taxes on the profits and come out with about $80,000.

That won't buy the house we had before, but we didn't need it anyway."

To conclude this particular couple's story, the bank to which Ron had been making the payments hired him to manage the fore-closed properties the bank had on its rolls. He did such a good job in that capacity that he was promoted to asset manager of the holding company's properties. Ron and Sue's children are still in the private school, and the couple has helped several other families attend the school through scholarships.

14
Learn to Live Within a Financial Plan

The financial troubles of the third couple discussed in this book, John and Mary Thompson, look at first as though they were the result of circumstances the couple could not control. Surely no one could have foreseen the medical problems their son would have or that the bills for his care would be so high. An argument could be made that the expenses they had with him would have wrecked anyone's budget.

But the fact is that Jack and Mary Thompson's financial troubles were the result of poor planning. Though they were intelligent and committed people, they had never been taught the basics of finances. They had never measured Jack's income against normal monthly expenses, and they had made no provision for any emergency spending they might someday have to make. The only way the couple made it financially was to use Mary's income to balance the budget.

This basic fact was not obvious to Jack and Mary and, as a consequence, the steps they took as they began to slip into debt were ones that made a bad situation worse.

Shortly after the baby was born, Jack and Mary's friends took up a collection to help them with the additional hospital expenses. However, the extent of the medical bills was far beyond the amount of money they had, and soon the bills were accumulating again. After meeting with the doctor, Jack talked with the hospital administrator. He recommended that the couple consider filing for bankruptcy. Two others, as well, counseled Jack to file for bankruptcy to relieve some of the financial pressure.

In the meantime, the couple found that they were unable to meet their mortgage payments and the payments on some furniture they had purchased. But since they had no real budget, they naturally assumed their financial problems were the result of the baby's medical expenses.

They soon began to develop an "I don't care" mentality about their finances. They assumed the situation was hopeless. They began to use their credit cards to fill the gaps in their budget. Jack bought his gas on credit and ate out on credit, while Mary bought baby supplies and food on credit. Without realizing it, they had adopted an attitude of despair and a philosophy that bankruptcy was inevitable. As is common, they were holding a pity party at their creditors' expense. With no visible means to repay, they were running up bills and living beyond their means. Although Jack would never have robbed a bank he was, in effect, doing the same thing—stealing from his creditors.

Seven months after the baby was born the couple was beginning to reap the seeds they had sown. Creditors were calling daily because nearly all their bills were delinquent. Two credit card companies had filed judgments against them, which Jack had ignored because he felt there was nothing that could be done anyway. When Jack's pay was garnished, he was called into the school administrator's office.

"Jack, I just received a notice of attachment from the court," Mr. Mills said solemnly. "I have to comply with the request and withhold 20 percent of your net pay. Do you have financial problems?"

"Yes sir," Jack responded a little defiantly. "It's the medical bills for the baby."

"We know the bills must be a problem for you and Mary, and we're working on something that might help. But the garnishment is the result of a judgment from a VISA bill. Is that related to the medical expenses?"

"No, not directly," Jack said, looking down at the floor as he spoke. "We've had to use our credit cards for normal expenses during the last few months. But it all started because of the baby's problems."

Then Mr. Mills began to realize that Jack had allowed the problems with the baby to distort his thinking. He said, "Jack, I believe you have more financial problems than just the medical bills from the baby. I know we don't pay our teachers nearly what the public school systems do, and it's tough to make it on one salary. But you took the job knowing that, and now I suspect that even without the baby you would be in over your head. I want you to go to a financial counselor and get a clear picture of where you are financially. There is a potentially embarrassing situation developing through this whole thing."

"How so, Mr. Mills?" Jack asked. "Will I lose my job over the garnishment?"

"No, Jack," Mr. Mills responded. "We have neither the right nor the authority to dismiss you for that reason. But with Mary not working, you would have a difficult time making ends meet even if all your finances were in perfect order. We do have some teachers supporting families on one salary, but they must be very careful and live on a strict budget. With this garnishment I know your budget won't make it. Do you have other debts besides the VISA?"

"Well, yes, we do," Jack responded uncomfortably.

"More than $1,000 worth?"

"Well, yes, I guess so. But we have decided to file for bankruptcy anyway. The medical bills would make it impossible to live on my salary no matter what," Jack said with an air of finality.

"No one could argue with that," Mr. Mills said as he recognized Jack's defensiveness. "But Jack, you and I have a responsibility to do what is right. You know, in the eyes of our generation, nothing is as visible as the way we handle our finances."

"I agree," Jack said, interrupting. "But do you think we chose this situation?"

"No, I'm sure you didn't, but, even if our roles were reversed and it was my son with the health problems, I still say you have allowed your circumstances to control you."

"That's easy for you to say, Mr. Mills, because it isn't your son, and you make more money than I do," Jack said defiantly.

"That's very true. But I would hope that our standard for life is not built on what someone else does or doesn't have or on what they would or wouldn't do in similar circumstances. You see, there will always be someone else who is better off than either of us and someone who has more money than both of us."

Again Jack said, "That's easy enough to say when it's not your finances. But I don't see anyone paying our bills for us."

"Perhaps that is not entirely true, Jack."

"What do you mean?"

"Several members of the school board and the faculty have put money in a trust fund for the medical bills you and Mary have incurred. We realize that you can't meet all your expenses. We have been paying something on the bills for the last two months now. Didn't you notice that the hospital and doctors had stopped sending you notices?"

Jack stopped cold. No, he hadn't noticed. He had been so caught up in his problems that he had taken an antagonistic stance in relation to most of the creditors and had ignored all of the notices they had been sending. Mary had commented several times that they should try to contact the major creditors and let them know that they were having some severe financial problems. Jack had shrugged it off saying, "We can't pay them anyway. So what difference does it make?"

"Another thing," Mr. Mills continued. "One of the school board members applied to a foundation that specializes in cases like yours. Notice just came in today that a grant has been approved that will pay all the medical bills and the cost of care that Johnny will need over the next several years."

Jack was taken aback for the second time that day. "I don't know what to say, Mr. Mills."

"You don't need to say anything. We did what we did because we care. But now I fear that you have positioned yourself so that just paying the medical bills won't solve the problems anymore. Let me encourage you to seek good counsel and not listen to the advice of those who look for the easy way out all the time."

Reality began to set in.

Jack was excited about going home and telling Mary the good news about the medical bills being taken care of by the foundation. But as he drove home, a feeling of depression came over him. He realized that they would still owe hundreds of dollars on the credit cards they had used during the last few months. He began to accept the fact that they would be paying for their ignorance and lack of self-discipline for a long time—perhaps for years.

Mary wasn't home when Jack arrived, so he decided to review some of the bills that had been sent during the last few weeks. Most of them were still in his desk drawer unopened. He opened the envelopes and began to sort the bills by date and amount. An hour passed as he sorted bills from oil company cards, department store cards, and three major credit cards. When he totaled what he had found, he was shocked. *Surely this must be some kind of mistake,* Jack told himself. *We can't possibly owe that much.*

Yet when he retotaled the stack, the figure came out the same: $6,764.34. Almost $7,000! And he knew that he still hadn't found all the bills. He had been so sure they only owed a few hundred dollars that even $1,000 would have been a shock. But $7,000. It seemed impossible.

When Mary arrived home, she knew immediately that something was wrong. Jack was still sitting at the desk looking at the stack of bills in front of him. "What's the problem, Jack?" she asked, not really wanting to know.

"I received word from Mr. Mills today that members of the school board have been paying on our medical bills. That's why we haven't been getting notices from the doctors or the hospital," he said.

"That's great," Mary responded enthusiastically. "But what's the problem?"

"That's not all, Mary," Jack continued in a somber mood. "Mr. Mills also said that a foundation has accepted all of Johnny's medical expenses from this point on. We won't have to pay anything except living expenses."

Mary was overwhelmed by the news. "Why, that's wonderful!"

"Not quite," Jack said "I just totaled up the credit card debts. We owe nearly $7,000, and I know that's not all of it."

"That's impossible," Mary nearly shouted.

"Unfortunately, it's not. We also have a judgment against my wages, as of today. I feel so stupid, Mary. I've been living as if there were no tomorrow. I guess I just assumed that we would have to go bankrupt, so I didn't care how much debt we ran up."

"What is our alternative now?" Mary asked as she moved to put Johnny in his crib.

"I believe we have only one. The debts we owe are a result of our own decisions, and I can't blame anyone but myself. I don't see how we can do anything but commit to paying all of our debts."

"But how will we be able to do that on your salary alone?" Mary asked.

"I don't think we can. I'll just have to tell Mr. Mills that I need to start looking for a new job. In the meantime I'll go to each of the creditors and ask for a reduced payment until I can generate more income. But we can't do much about the garnishment. That will come out of each paycheck until the bill is paid in full. It won't leave us a lot to live on, but we'll have to learn to do it.

"I want to cut up the credit cards, too. As long as we have them, we'll be tempted to use them. And I think we need to go back to driving one car. Maybe we can sell my car for enough money to clear the VISA and the garnishment."

"But, Jack, my car has nearly one hundred thousand miles on it. Can we get by with a car that old?"

"We'll have to, Mary. It's going to be tough for a while, but as I said, we'll just have to do it."

Jack left the private school for a job as a teacher and coach at a public school. He and Mary went to see the counselor Mr. Mills had suggested and worked out a plan with the creditors that allowed them some transition time. It was nearly two years before they began to see daylight in their finances, but in three years they were totally debt-free.

15

Accept Responsibility for Your Life

In this chapter I would like to look at another couple, Bill and Pam. They were both in their early twenties and in college, both came out of middle-class homes, and both attended public schools most of their lives. Neither Bill nor Pam had ever attended a course on personal finances, and although they had both worked at a variety of summer jobs for several years, neither had more than a general idea of how to balance a checkbook.

They met at a campus rally and kept steady company thereafter. Both Pam and Bill were attending college on a variety of loans and grants available to them. By their senior year their loans totaled nearly $8,000 each. Bill knew he would be expected to repay his loans after graduation because his dad had made that clear from the beginning. Since he felt he had little choice, he continued to accumulate school loans.

Pam and her parents never discussed the repayment of the loans she was receiving. She assumed that her dad would pay them, as he had all of her bills, but she never really gave it much thought. But then, in the early part of her senior year, Pam's father died of a sudden heart attack. Her mother was devastated by her loss and went into a prolonged state of depression. Pam dropped out of school for one quarter and then returned to finish her degree. In the past, her father had always given her money for the incidentals she needed just before she left for school. Since her father was gone, Pam approached her mother.

"Mom, I'll need some money for books and dorm fees," she said.

"Dad always handled the finances, honey. I don't know what you need. Why don't you take my credit cards and get whatever is necessary. We'll work it out when you come home next time. Maybe Daddy's insurance will be settled by that time, and I'll know what we have."

Pam's mom then handed her two credit cards, one for buying gas for her car and the other for general expenses. Although Pam had never owned a card of her own, she had often used her mother's to fill up the family car or run errands for her mom. The cards had only her mother's initials and last name on them. Because Pam had the same initials as her mother, the merchants never questioned her signature.

Back at school, Pam called home regularly to see how her mom was doing. She was still in a state of semi-shock and was virtually unaware that Pam called her almost every day. When the first month's phone bill came for Pam's dorm phone, it was nearly $200. She paid it with the card her mother had given her.

Pam needed some clothes for school and normally would have called and asked her dad for some money. Usually he sent her a check for $100 or so, and she would buy a pair of jeans and a blouse or two. Since she knew her mother was in no shape to answer questions, she decided to use the card this time. By the time she finished the shopping trip, she had charged over $500 worth of new clothes and had also charged a watch for Bill for another $120.

She and Bill had begun talking seriously about their plans after graduation. They knew they would get married, but beyond that had no definite plans for what they would do. Pam's degree in elementary education required her to intern for at least three months; then her employment would depend on finding an opening in the school system near the college. Bill was earning a degree in music and wanted to go on to graduate school to gain his master's degree so he could teach music at the college level.

During the next three months, Pam fell into a routine of using her mother's credit card periodically to take Bill out to eat and buy him gifts. Then her car broke down, and she had the brakes fixed—again using the card. Without realizing it she began to develop a habit of small indulgences, using her mother's card to pay for them. None were particularly significant by themselves but, when totaled, they began to add up. The bills came to her mother's home where she put them on her desk and left them unopened. She couldn't cope with the details of daily life yet.

Suddenly Pam saw school coming to an end and was faced with entering the work force for the first time. She began to feel a little panicked herself. She thought more and more about getting married. She feared that, if they waited until summer, something might happen to keep them from getting married; that thought really panicked her. She had lost her father; she couldn't stand the thought of possibly losing Bill, too.

One evening she said to Bill, "Why don't we go ahead and get married? I know Mom is in no shape to take on a wedding, and I'm not sure she could emotionally handle seeing me get married anyway."

"But how will we make it financially?" Bill asked. "Neither of us has a job, and you still have your student teaching to complete."

"We already have my apartment," Pam replied, "and without your dorm fee our expenses would actually be less, wouldn't they?"

"Well, I guess so," he replied as he thought about the idea. "But I don't know if my dad would continue to pay my bills if I got married."

"We should be able to qualify for some grants if we're married," Pam responded enthusiastically. "And besides, we'll have your student loans while you're in grad school."

The more Bill thought about the idea, the more he liked it too. Graduation was only two months away, and then Pam would be finished. They had planned to get married that next summer anyway, so what difference would three or four months make?

Besides, he thought. *Pam's right. Her mother is certainly in no shape to go through a wedding.* "I think it's a great idea," he said as he put his arms around her. "When would you like to get married?"

"What about right now?" she asked.

"Right now?" Bill echoed as he looked at his watch. "But it's nearly eleven o'clock, and we have classes tomorrow. Besides, we have to wait at least three days for the blood tests."

"We could miss Friday's classes," she argued, a little hurt that Bill was hesitating. "And we can always drive to another state where there is no waiting period."

"But Pam, the nearest state is Virginia, and that's nearly two hundred miles. I don't even have gas money right now."

"I've got my credit cards," she responded eagerly. "It wouldn't cost that much. It would be like a little honeymoon."

Bill had a nagging feeling inside about doing something this serious on impulse. He wondered what his mom would say when she found out. But seeing Pam so excited, and knowing that they did love each other, he could come up with no logical arguments that would satisfy her. So he said, "Okay Pam, we'll get married. You pack some things, and I'll call my mom and let her know."

Pam panicked inside as Bill mentioned calling his mom. "Please don't tell anyone right now," she pleaded. "They'll just try to talk us out of it. I want this to be our surprise. We'll tell them after graduation, okay?"

Bill agreed reluctantly, but he knew his mom would be hurt when she found out. Pam said, "Let's just go like we are. We don't need any extra clothes. We'll only be gone two days at the most, and we can buy something if we really need it."

By this time Bill was totally into the idea as well, so he replied, "This is really crazy, but if that's what you want, honey, we'll do it. At least we'll have something to tell our grandchildren. But let's agree on one thing. No children until we're both out of school and settled into our jobs. Okay?"

Pam agreed and grabbed Bill around the waist. "We're going to be so happy, Bill. I just know it."

Bill and Pam took off for Virginia. Four hours later they stopped to eat a very late dinner. While they were eating, they mentioned to the waitress that they were driving to Virginia to get married the next day.

"Do you have your license yet?" she asked.

"No," Bill replied. "We understand we don't have to wait in Virginia."

"Well, I don't know who told you that, honey," she said in a deep Southern drawl. "But it simply ain't true. You gotta wait at least two days."

"We can't wait," Pam said in alarm. "We have to be back in school Monday morning."

"Well, I'd suggest you go to New Jersey then," the waitress said authoritatively. "You don't have to wait at all up there. That's where we got married a few years back."

"We can't drive all the way to New Jersey," Bill argued. "It would take ten or twelve more hours."

"But we can't just turn around and go back home," Pam complained. "We've already come this far. Let's go on, please."

Bill was in no mood to discuss anything objectively, and when he saw the hurt on Pam's face, he surrendered. "Okay," he said. "If you're willing, I am too. But let's get going. We'll just make it back in time."

Pam had literally jumped out of her seat and was headed toward the door when Bill asked, "Do you have any cash, Pam? I'm a little short to pay the bill."

Pam dug into her purse and found about three dollars in change. She asked the waitress, "Can I pay for the meal with my credit card?"

"Sorry, honey," the waitress replied, "the boss won't let us take credit cards. He says they cost him too much."

So Bill paid the check with what he and Pam could scrape together, and they headed toward New Jersey. Several hours later they entered New Jersey and encountered their first toll bridge. In the meantime their periodic stops had exhausted their small cash reserve. The toll gate attendant told them that they would either have to pay the toll or turn around and go back.

"Can we pay the toll with a credit card?" Pam asked.

"No, you can't, miss," he answered. "Look, kids, the toll is only $1.10. Are you telling me you don't even have that much on you?"

Looking a little sheepish Bill replied, "I'm afraid not. You see, we were planning to get married in Virginia, but when we found out we had to wait two days, we decided to drive up here instead. We have to be back in school Monday."

"Well, good luck. But I don't think you're getting off to a good start this way. Exactly how much do you have?"

"About fifty-six cents," Pam said in a whisper.

"Tell you what I'll do," the attendant said in a stern voice. "Give me what you have, and I'll put in the difference. You're holding up traffic."

"Oh, thank you, sir," was Pam's reply.

"Just one thing," the man said. "How are you planning to get back across?"

Bill was suddenly struck by the same thought. "How are we going to get back across with no money?"

"I have an aunt who lives not far from here," Pam volunteered. "We'll go see her. I'm sure she will help."

With a sinking feeling inside, Bill drove across the bridge and into New Jersey. He realized that what they were doing didn't make any sense, but he didn't know what else to do. Pam was totally committed to the idea of marriage. He was too, but he had some reservations about the timing.

They drove to Pam's aunt's home. She was speechless when Pam called her to say they were only a couple of miles away. But she asked them to come over and began to prepare some lunch.

When Pam and Bill rang the doorbell, she opened it to find two worn out and totally rumpled young people. "Pam, come in," she said. "Who is your young man, and what in the world brings you here?"

"This is Bill, Aunt Maye," she said. "We're getting married and just dropped by to see you."

"Getting married?" Pam's aunt said with surprise. "Does your mom know about this?"

"No, ma'am. She's really been depressed since Daddy's death, and we thought it would be better to elope and not put her through the stress of a wedding."

"Well, I can't argue that she's in no shape for any more emotional trauma," her aunt said. "But I don't know that running away to get married is the right answer, either. Do your parents know, Bill?"

"No, ma'am," he replied shyly. "But we are of legal age, and my folks know we plan to get married in the summer."

"Then why all the rush?" she asked.

Pam jumped in, "We just believe that this is what we should do, Aunt Maye. But we have a little problem and wondered if you could help."

"What kind of problem, dear?"

"We've had to drive further than we planned and ran out of cash. I wondered if you would mind cashing a small check for me?"

"I don't want your check, dear. I'll be glad to give you some money as a wedding present. But I certainly wish you would think about this some more."

"We have already thought about it, and we know this is what we want to do," Pam said emphatically. Bill started to answer but changed his mind. Then Pam's aunt said something that set them both back.

"But I don't understand why you drove all the way up here. New Jersey has a three-day waiting period before you can get married."

"That can't be," Pam said almost in hysteria. "A waitress in Virginia said she got married here without a wait."

"That must have been some time ago," her aunt said. "I'll call and check for you, but I'm sure that's right."

A brief call to the local justice of the peace confirmed her statement. "He says the closest place to get married with no wait is Virginia."

"That's impossible," Bill moaned. "We were just there and that waitress told us that Virginia has a waiting period, too."

Another long distance call to the sheriff's department in Lynch County, Virginia, confirmed that they could get married without a wait if they were of legal age.

"I suspect the waitress thought you kids were not old enough to get married without permission," Aunt Maye said. "And she probably had someone pull some strings for her here. I'm afraid you'll just have to wait until you get back to Virginia."

They decided to sleep a few hours before they headed back, and in the interim Pam's aunt washed and dried their well-worn clothes. Four hours later they were back on the road, headed toward Virginia, where they finally were married by a justice of the peace. By that time they were totally broke and running out of time before classes started.

"That'll be $10," the justice said. "And $10 more for the license."

"Will you take a credit card?" Pam asked meekly.

"Sorry, honey, cash only," the justice responded rather brusquely.

"But we don't have any cash," Pam pleaded. "Will you take a check?"

"I normally take cash only. It's Saturday night and nobody can cash your check until Monday. You kids don't have any money at all?" he asked looking at Bill.

"No, sir," Bill replied.

"Well, I guess I'll have to take a check then," he said irritably. "But I'll need some collateral. I've been stiffed by too many of you college kids already."

"What kind of collateral?" Pam asked nervously. She knew that if they didn't get a license they weren't legally married.

"I'll take that Seiko you're wearing," he told Bill, pointing at his watch.

"But that's brand new," Pam protested. "And it was a gift from me."

"Well, take it or leave it," the justice said gruffly. "Otherwise you can wait until Monday and cash your check at the bank."

"No, we can't wait," Bill said as he removed the watch. "Can we get it back after the check clears?"

"Why sure, kids. You just drop me a note, and I'll send it right along," he said with a chuckle.

A month later Pam's mother called her. "Pam, I've been looking through some of the bills from my bank, and I see that the credit card is over the limit. I called our banker, and he said he had allowed the overdraft because he knew about Daddy's death and figured I was waiting on the insurance payment. But Pam, I haven't used that card much at all, and it has more than $4,000 charged on it."

"Four thousand dollars! Mother, that's impossible," Pam exclaimed. "I've used it for school expenses and some clothes, but I certainly didn't charge $4,000!"

"And the Gulf card has $840 on it, Pam. Have you used it? There are charges on here from Virginia, Delaware, New Jersey, and who knows where else. Did you drive up to New Jersey recently?"

Pam sat quietly for a few seconds. She was overwhelmed by the news from her mother. She had put the trip and the charges completely out of her mind during the last month. Being married was everything to her, and she and Bill had been very happy, but now she knew she had to tell her mother that they were married. "Mom, Bill and I got married a month ago. That's where the gas charges came from. But don't worry, we'll pay you back."

Pam's mother had already put two and two together and suspected something like that. She replied, "That was your choice, honey, but I wish you had at least let me know before you got married. Bill's mother is going to be very upset. Of course, you'll have to work that out for yourselves. You know, your dad and I always said that when you got married you would have to manage your own household. I'm sending all the bills to you. You'll have to take care of them."

"But Mom," she pleaded, "we don't have the money to pay all the bills right now. I'm student teaching, and Bill is getting ready for his finals next month."

"I'm sorry, Pam, but you should have considered that before you got married and ran up those bills." With that, she hung up the phone.

Pam looked around the small room that served as their living area. There sat the television and stereo she had charged on the credit card before she and Bill were married, and she realized that she may very well have charged $4,000—and more. She had been using the card since they got married and was frightened as she realized that probably they had charged another several hundred dollars.

Graduation was still five weeks away, and they had no visible means of support. She decided not to tell Bill anything about what her mother had said until after graduation. He needed to concentrate on graduating, and she knew he would worry himself sick about the bills. He already looked haggard from concern over what he would tell his parents.

For nearly two weeks Pam tried diligently not to use the credit card for anything. Her mother had sent her the bills and, after looking through them, she knew they were her charges. Then one evening while Bill was in a class she got a call from Bill's mother.

"Pam, is Bill home?" she asked. Without thinking Pam replied, "No, he's still in class."

There was a long pause on the other end of the line. Pam tried to think of something to say, but decided that this was as good a time as any for Bill's mother to find out.

"Are you and Bill living together?" Bill's mother asked with a measured calmness.

"Well, Mrs. Yates, we got married about a month ago,' Pam replied. "I'm sorry we didn't tell you, but we just didn't know how."

"We knew something was wrong when the school wrote and told us Bill had moved out of the dorm," she said sternly. "I do think you both owed us enough respect to tell us yourselves. But if you're married, you're married, so let's make the best of it. Please tell Bill to call me when he comes in. We would like for you both to come down for a day as soon as you can."

"We will, I promise," Pam replied. "And we're very happy, Mrs. Yates. We do love each other, and we didn't do this to hurt anyone."

"Pam, you're a member of our family now, and we love you too. But I'm disappointed that you didn't trust us enough to believe we would allow you to make your own decisions. You can't start a relationship with an attitude of distrust. Please remember that in your marriage, too."

When she hung up, Pam sat still for several minutes. What Bill's mother had said hit her in a sensitive spot. She knew they had been deceitful to their parents, and she knew she had been deceiving Bill. It had gone on so long now she was wondering how he would react when he finally knew the whole truth. When Bill came home, she told him about his mother's call. He looked like he was going to be sick for a minute. Then he said, "I don't blame her for being hurt and angry. I know I have been lying to them since we got married. I'd better call her and at least let her know I'm sorry."

"I'm sorry, Bill," Pam said honestly. "I suppose I'm the one at fault. You wanted to call her and I talked you out of it. I was afraid she would convince you not to get married."

"No, Pam, I'm the one at fault. I know I'm supposed to be the leader in our home. If I had had the courage, I would have been honest with my parents up front. I just hope this doesn't affect our relationship with them from now on."

After a brief conversation with his mother and his father, Bill hung up the phone. "Well, they're both hurt," he said. "But they both want you to know they're glad to have you as a member of our family, and they will make the best of the situation. My dad said that we'll have to come up with the money for grad school ourselves. He believes we should stand on our own two feet. I guess that means I'll have to put it off for a while—at least until we can save a little money."

"What about graduation expenses and the school loans?" Pam asked apprehensively. She had intended to tell Bill about the other debts, but now she wondered if she should.

"He said he'll continue to pay until I graduate, and they're going to give us a $500 wedding gift to help us get started. The school loans are mine to pay, but I knew that from the beginning."

Pam decided she would wait to tell Bill about the debts until he had a chance to recover from the shock of telling his parents. The opportunity didn't come up again before graduation and, with the $500 from Bill's parents, they were able to get by for the next month.

Bill found a job selling records in a music store. Although it didn't pay much, he figured he could find something better after the summer break when all the other students went back to school.

One evening Bill answered the doorbell and there stood Pam's mother. "Mrs. Carlisle, come in. What are you doing over here?" he asked.

"Bill, I need to talk with you and Pam about something urgent. Is she here?"

"Yes, she is," he replied. At that moment Pam came through the door from the bedroom saying, "Who's at the door, Bill?" When she saw her mother, she paled to the point of looking ashen.

"Mother, what are you doing here?" she asked in a hollow voice.

"Pam, you know very well what I'm doing here," her mother answered. "It's about these." With that, she thrust a handful of credit card receipts in front of her. "You told me you were going to take care of these, and now I have received notice that the bank is filing suit against me."

"What are those?" Bill asked as Pam made her way to the living room couch, nearly collapsing.

"They're bills run up on my credit cards," Pam's mother said in an accusing tone. "Didn't Pam tell you I called her about them nearly two months ago?"

Bill looked over at Pam. One glance told him the answer. "No, she didn't," he said. "But if they're our bills, I give you my word we'll pay every one of them, Mrs. Carlisle."

"Well, I hope you will," she replied as she headed toward the front door again. "I want you both to know how disappointed I am that you started out this way. It's partly my fault too. Apparently we didn't teach Pam some things she needed to know, especially about handling money. We never had very much ourselves and always lived on what little we had. I guess we just assumed our daughter would know how to do the same."

With that she walked over to Pam, who was crying softly, and hugged her. "I love you, honey, but you need to grow up. When you take on the rights of an adult, you also take on the responsibilities. I can't pay these bills, but I wouldn't even if I could. You need to accept the consequences of your actions, Pam. And you need to be totally honest with your husband," she said in a solemn tone.

After Pam's mother left, Bill sat down to talk with her about the bills. "How much do we really owe, Pam?" he asked with as much control as possible.

"I don't know," she replied. "I haven't added up all the bills yet. I'm sorry for not telling you before. I didn't want to bother you during your finals, and then I was afraid to tell you."

"Pam, you don't need to be afraid to tell me anything. But we do need to figure out exactly how much we owe and how we're going to pay."

After two hours of pouring over the bills that had come in and estimating those which had not been sent yet, Bill came up with a figure of nearly $5,000 between the gas card and the bank card.

"What are we going to do?" she asked Bill.

"I don't know right now," he answered. "But grad school is out for the fall. And I'm going to need to look for a better job, or we'll be going further in the hole each month."

"I can get a job, too," Pam offered. "I complete my internship in a little more than a week. But school doesn't start again for nearly three months, so I won't know about a teaching job for a month or more."

"Pam, we're both going to have to make some sacrifices to pay these debts," Bill said. "I've really been foolish not to see that we were living over our heads. I guess I didn't want to know. I'm going to call Ken Riggs at the bank tomorrow to see if he knows anyone who can help us work out a plan."

The next day Bill stopped by to see the banker and told him the overview of what had happened. "Unfortunately, Bill, what has happened to you and Pam is not unusual today. Too much credit is put in the hands of young people who have little or no idea how to control their use of it. I'm sure Pam was as shocked as her mother to find out how much she had spent."

"There's no question about that, Ken," Bill responded, "but I need to know what we can do about it. We'll pay back everything in time, but right now it looks kind of hopeless."

"It's never hopeless if you're willing to admit your mistakes and correct them," Ken Riggs commented. "I want you to call one of our staff who volunteers with a local financial counseling program. He'll work out a time to meet with you and Pam."

Bill immediately called Chris Wilson, the one that Ken Riggs referred him to. "I'll be glad to see you and Pam this evening, Bill. I'll meet you at my office at eight o'clock, if that's okay with you."

"That will be fine, Mr. Wilson," Bill responded. "And thank you for taking the time."

"Don't mention it. That's my area of service to our community. See you tonight at eight."

At eight o'clock Bill and Pam were waiting outside the impressive office building. Chris Wilson arrived, and Bill recognized him from a meeting he had attended more than a year ago, in which Mr. Wilson had spoken on the need for young people to be good managers of their credit. *I sure wish I had listened better,* Bill said to himself.

Bill and Pam described the events of the past several months that had brought them to the point where they were. Chris Wilson made several notes as they discussed the particular events.

"As I see it," he said, "you have several symptoms and two basic problems."

"What do you mean, Mr. Wilson?" Pam asked. "What's the difference?"

"The problems created the symptoms," he responded. "For instance, you now owe nearly $5,000 in consumer debt. But that's a symptom of a much deeper problem, I believe. If your parents just gave you the money to pay the bills, I believe they would be doing you a disservice, because it's likely that you would repeat the same mistakes again."

"Not me," Pam said emphatically.

"I know that's what you think right now, Pam," he said. "And probably you wouldn't repeat the exact same mistakes. But indulgence comes in many forms, and future mistakes can create much more severe consequences. I've seen people making more than $100,000 a year get deeply into debt because their impulses grew even faster than their salaries.

"I think I can help you get out from under the circumstances if you're willing to sacrifice for a while. But unless you recognize the problems and solve them, you'll be back again."

"What do you think the problems are, Mr. Wilson?" Bill asked.

"As I see it, Bill, your problem stems from a lack of self-confidence. But it shows itself in the fact that you haven't accepted your role as the head of your family."

"What do you mean?"

"First you allowed yourself to be led into a quick elopement and, because you didn't want to hurt Pam's feelings, you weren't honest with her. No sound relationship can ever be built on a foundation of fear."

"But I don't want to dictate to Pam," Bill argued. Even as he said it he knew somewhere deep inside that what Mr. Wilson had said was right. He did fear losing Pam, and that was his prime motivation the weekend they eloped. He had seen the foolishness of what they were doing even from the beginning, but he didn't have the courage to tell her no.

"I don't mean that you should dictate to your wife, Bill; she is to be your partner. But Pam has the stronger personality, and she will tend to set the pace."

"But, Mr. Wilson, I don't want to lead Bill around," Pam protested. "I want to be a good wife and a helpmate."

"Yes, and I believe you do, Pam, or I wouldn't have brought this up so bluntly on our first visit. But you need to realize that you have a more dominant personality and you must learn to control it."

"Is that the second problem then?" she asked meekly.

"No, the second problem you need to deal with is your indulgent attitude," Mr. Wilson said candidly.

"What?" Pam said as she came out of her chair. "I don't think I have an indulgent attitude. I've never wasted money before this."

"But Pam, you never had the opportunity before," Mr. Wilson said as she sat back down. "From what you said, I suspect that your dad ran your home and doled out the money he wanted you to have. And he was probably pretty cautious with his money, wasn't he?"

"Well, yes," Pam agreed. "I never thought about me having an indulgent attitude."

"Some of the spending was ignorance about credit cards. But when the totals come to $5,000, it usually goes far beyond just simple ignorance," Mr. Wilson said. "Some people have such an indulgent attitude they can't pass by anything they don't already have. It's almost an obsession. Often it's not even for themselves; they'll even buy gifts for other people using their credit cards."

Pam thought about the watch she had bought for Bill. She had bought him another one two weeks after they returned home from getting married. Bill had protested but she'd convinced him to keep it.

Mr. Wilson continued, "We all like to buy things, and we can all indulge, given the opportunity and the resources. But some people are what I would call shop-a-holics. They feel best when they're buying something, even if they know they can't afford it."

Pam realized that much of what the counselor was saying did apply to her. She never had splurged very much, but she hadn't had the opportunity until she had gotten her mother's credit card. Then it became a need that she had to satisfy. She had felt the same way about getting married that weekend. She didn't think she was going to lose Bill, but she wasn't willing to take the chance.

"Does that mean I should never handle the money again?" Pam asked dejectedly.

"Not at all. It just means that you need to realize that Bill is in your life to offset your imbalances, just as you are to offset his. When you recognize what those imbalances are and learn to communicate about them openly, you'll be further along than 90 percent of the couples today.

"In the meantime we need to deal with the immediate problem —these debts. I notice in your list of assets that you own two cars. Is that right?"

"Yes, sir," Bill said. "Pam's and mine."

"How much do you think they're worth, Bill?"

"I would say mine is worth $1,500—$1,600 at best—and Pam's is worth $1,000," Bill replied.

"And I see that you have a stereo and television. Anything else of any substantial value, like an insurance policy or stocks?"

"No, sir," Bill replied again, "just the normal junk furniture that most college students accumulate over the years."

"Bill, I do have a small insurance policy that Daddy bought for me when I was a little girl," Pam said.

"Do you know if it has any cash value, Pam?" Mr. Wilson asked.

"I think so. I had forgotten that I even had it until you mentioned the insurance. Daddy said it would pay either a lump sum or provide enough for burial, but I don't know how much."

"Okay, what we have to work with, then, is the potential sale of one car, a stereo, TV, and some cash in an insurance policy."

"But Mr. Wilson, we need both of our cars if we're both going to work," Pam argued. "Bill works in one direction, and I work in another."

"I know it won't be easy, but it is possible. You both need to be totally realistic about your situation, and since we don't have a lot of leeway in time, I'm going to lay it out for you. I hope this doesn't frighten you off, but you need to face reality.

"First, the bank has already started action against Pam's mother. In less than two weeks there will be a court hearing, and I feel sure the judge will grant the petition to attach her property unless we can work out another arrangement in the meantime.

"Second, even without the debts, you're living beyond your means right now. You can't afford a second car. It takes extra insurance, maintenance, and gas.

"Third, I assume that the stereo and TV were bought with the credit card, so you need to sell them and return the money to the bank. Obviously you won't get back what you paid, but that's the way it is usually.

"Even after you do these things, your budget won't balance while you're paying off the remaining debts unless you both work. That means you have another choice to make. Pam, you will have to find a job as soon as possible, and Bill, you'll have to find another job with a more stable income."

"We already decided to do that," Bill offered. "And I realize that I won't be able to go to grad school in the fall."

"Not necessarily," Mr. Wilson said. "If you could live with one set of parents and go to school closer to home, it might be possible to at least start evening classes."

"I don't know about that," Bill said. "I think both of our parents are peeved at us right now."

"Do you really blame them?" Mr. Wilson said. "So far you have gotten married on an impulse, failed to tell the people who love you the most, charged $5,000 on someone else's credit card, and have a bank in your hometown ready to sue your mother."

"I guess when you look at it that way, we do look a little juvenile, don't we?" Pam said.

"To say the least," Mr. Wilson agreed. "Now it's time to start applying some financial principles."

"What do you mean?" Bill asked.

"Principle number one is to sell whatever you don't actually need to live and give the money to your creditors.

"Principle number two is to go to your creditors and ask their forgiveness. Then work out a repayment plan with them.

"And the last principle you need to apply is to think and plan before you act. From this point on, you both need to vow that you won't make impetuous decisions and that you will make every decision after discussing it thoroughly.

"Pam, you have been blessed with an ability to lead and direct. Those qualities will be very beneficial both in your career and in your role as a homemaker. But you must be willing to cooperate as a team, with Bill at the head.

"Now I'd like for you both to contact the bank and the credit manager for the oil company and work out a repayment plan. Tell them you're in the process of selling some assets and will pay them that money up front. Feel free to tell them you're working with me; they can call me for verification. And one more thing. I will do everything I can to help you get out of this situation, but you must agree to develop a budget together and stick to it diligently during this process. If not, I will spend my time with those who are willing to listen."

"Mr. Wilson, I promise we'll stick to the plan. I want to get out of this mess and get our lives back on track," Bill said.

"And how about you, Pam?" Mr. Wilson asked.

"I want to get out of this mess, naturally," Pam responded. "But I am really afraid that what you said about my being an impulse spender is true. What if I can't control myself and do this again?"

"Pam, spending is not like alcoholism or drug addiction, although it can be if you don't exercise self-control. You need to establish some guidelines for yourself that include relying on Bill to balance your extremes. Once you make a budget, don't violate it. That doesn't mean you can't ever spend any money or that you won't need some free money for your own use. Everybody does. But limit yourself to what you can afford, and don't rely on credit cards to fill in the gaps. Credit makes it too easy to splurge and is too difficult to pay back. If you stick to your repayment plan, you'll be out of debt in a short while, perhaps even in a few months. But if you don't, you may well find yourselves included in those unfortunate divorce statistics. Nearly half of all new marriages fail, and the vast majority claim that financial problems caused their marital problems."

"I can believe that," Bill said. "I don't know what we would have done if it weren't for you, Mr. Wilson. I really was beginning to feel the pressure."

"I haven't done anything but help you realize that there are answers to your problems. Now it's up to you to work out the details and stick to them. I'll give you some materials that will help you understand the basic principles. These must be your guide if you want to make good decisions in the future. You need to learn how to keep a checkbook accurately and keep up with your monthly budget. We'll work that out together over the next few weeks."

Bill and Pam called the vice president of the bank in charge of credit card accounts and asked for a meeting the next day. They told him exactly what had happened and asked if they could work out a repayment plan. He agreed to convert the credit card debt into a personal loan collateralized by both of their cars. The next month Bill's car was sold, and they were able to pay the $1,800 they received toward the loan amount.

Pam sold the stereo and television and got another $1,200 to pay on the loan. Within a few weeks they had the loan amount down to less than $2,000. With the help of Mr. Wilson, they worked out a repayment plan with the oil company so they could pay the minimum amount until the bank loan was repaid. The cash from the insurance policy reduced the loan by another $500.

Bill took a job with a national delivery service that paid nearly twice what he had been making. Pam took a job in telephone sales and found that she really enjoyed the work. Between the two of them, they were able to pay off the bank loan in five months, although it meant a lot of scrimping and early mornings, as Bill would drop Pam off at her job and then drive across town to his. But after three months, Bill's employer allowed him to drive the company delivery van home in the evenings. That not only provided them a second vehicle, nearly cost-free, but also lowered their gas bill considerably.

Once the bank loan was totally paid off, Bill approached the loan officer about borrowing enough to eliminate the other credit card debt, which carried a 21 percent interest rate. The banker agreed, based on their recent track record, and they substituted a 12 percent loan for the higher one.

In the fall, Pam accepted a teaching position with a private school, and they began to settle into a reasonably normal routine. Over the course of three months they counseled with Mr. Wilson once a week. During that time they learned how to balance and maintain their checking account and how to develop a realistic budget. In the fourth month Mr. Wilson called Bill to ask if he and Pam would be willing to meet and counsel another young couple. Bill asked Pam, who wholeheartedly agreed, and they began their first one-on-one counseling to help another couple.

Bill ultimately earned his master's degree and went on to get a Ph.D. in music. He now heads a department at the university where he and Pam attended school. They lived with Pam's mother for about a year and a half, during which time they helped her to get started on a budget. During that time she also trained for her new career in nursing, which she could afford to do only because of their financial assistance for nearly four years.

Bill and Pam's financial recovery was possible only because they faced their problems honestly and worked through them together.

16

Three Major Expenses That Lead to Debt

As our look at four couples has demonstrated, a common thread in most of their experiences was the lack of thorough planning. Sometimes this flaw is amplified by ignorance or indulgence but, without some kind of financial plan (budget), most couples won't realize they have a problem until it overwhelms them.

Many couples think they live on a budget because they write down their check amounts and even balance their checking accounts. That is not a budget. A budget balances income and expenses and reports on the status of those each month. I'm not going to discuss the subject of budgeting here because I have done so in several previous books, including a thorough plan outlined in *The Financial Planning Workbook* (Chicago: Moody, 1982). Instead, I am going to discuss some of the more common ways couples get into debt.

The Purchase of a Home

Nearly every young couple in America dreams of owning their own home. I use the term "owning" loosely here because what that means to most couples is to be paying a mortgage. So the common definition of owning is "as opposed to renting." Many couples try to buy a home too soon or pay too much and end up in financial trouble. Unfortunately, quite often they don't realize that owning the home created their financial troubles because it took too large a portion of their spendable income. Just as with Paul and Julie, the first couple discussed in this book, they find themselves falling further behind every month.

The percentage of an average family's budget that should be spent on a house payment is no more than 25 percent of net spendable income (after charitable giving and taxes). Add to the mortgage payments the cost of utilities, insurance, maintenance, and incidentals, and the percentage climbs to around 35 or 36 percent. Unfortunately many couples commit more than 60 percent of their budget to housing. There is virtually no way to handle that kind of cost. If they plan their spending as a whole for the year, the strain would be apparent. But because they usually look only at one month, they don't see it. The monthly budget that couples typically work out usually lacks allocations for clothes, car repairs, and medical expenses. So it is unrealistic.

If you can afford to purchase a home within your budget, that makes sense. But if you wreck your budget just to get into a home, that makes no sense at all. The compulsion Americans have for buying large, expensive homes is just a reflection of poor planning in general. Most couples would be far better off saving for a down payment of at least 20 percent and buying a smaller, less expensive home initially. Certainly the purchase of a home for a young couple should never be determined on the basis of their combined incomes, for if one income fails (for example, if the wife becomes pregnant and she has to stay home with the child), the entire purchase will be in jeopardy. That violates the principle of good planning.

Andy and Bea did what most young couples do within the first five years of their marriage: they bought a home based on two incomes, and even then it stretched their budget. Bea got pregnant and was unable to work regularly, so they fell steadily behind on their bills. Within a few months she was juggling payments, based on which creditor was threatening legal action. The stress on Bea threatened her pregnancy and made her even more miserable. The doctor feared she might lose the baby and ordered her to bed for complete rest. But the problems didn't ease; they intensified because of the greater financial drain.

Andy found himself resentful of the fact that Bea couldn't work, and often they would end the evening sleeping in separate rooms in their "dream house." Andy also found himself using his credit cards to buy gas and other basic necessities because he was so low on cash. As a result of a seminar they attended at their church, they recognized a need for help, and they called for an appointment.

The home they had bought consumed nearly 70 percent of Andy's take-home pay. It was obvious that it was totally beyond their financial ability. When I pointed this out, Bea became very defensive. She was not willing to discuss the prospect of selling the home, and Andy was extremely uncomfortable even talking about it.

Bea had grown up as a preacher's kid, and when her father was killed in an automobile accident, her family was put out of the manse within a month. They were left homeless and nearly destitute for several years. That experience had left such a mark on Bea that she almost had a paranoia about selling her home.

The couple left that day with the details of how to establish a budget that would allocate something for every category of spending. In addition, they were asked to determine how much money they could free up to begin repaying some of the existing debt.

When they returned in two weeks the answer was clear. When the house payment had been made, there was nothing left over to pay bills. In fact, the true monthly deficit was close to $300. They had tried to discuss the issue of the home as I had suggested but it always ended with Bea crying, so Andy avoided the subject entirely. They both wanted to do what was right but were stymied by something as material as a house.

Bea had great difficulty with the idea of giving up her home. She was intelligent and realized that the home was beyond their means at that time but, as with any other paranoia, if it made sense it wouldn't have been a paranoia. I was convinced that neither I nor anyone else was going to talk her into voluntarily selling her home. She dug in her heels like an agoraphobic being dragged onto an elevator. Although selling their home might be the best thing for her, she couldn't see it that way at all.

The one thing Bea did agree with was the fact that the house was too expensive for their budget and that month by month the situation would get worse if they didn't do something. At that point the decision had to be Bea's.

A few weeks later she called back tearfully to report that their financial situation had deteriorated. Andy had made a commitment not to use the credit cards and actually had cut them up. Shortly after he did so, the car broke down. Having no money for repairs, he decided to park the car and hitch rides to and from work. Their Sunday school class heard about this from a friend and took up a donation to get the car repaired. In fact, they even raised a small surplus of funds, and the class asked Andy to use it to take Bea out for an evening.

That made a great impact on Bea. She realized that even though she hated to see Andy struggling to find rides to and from work, she still had regarded the house discussion as off limits. The house had become her idol.

When they came in for the next session, Bea had already put the house up for sale and had a tentative offer. I don't think she was jubilant about the decision, but she was resolved. I doubt if I could have talked her out of selling the home if I had tried, which I didn't.

Several weeks later their home sold, and the equity from the sale cleared all the bills. They moved into a duplex, which they shared with an elderly couple. Almost one year after they had sold their home, a member of their church called them. He was moving to Europe for several years and wanted to keep the home he lived in, since it had been in his family for several generations, but he didn't want to leave it vacant. The company he worked for was willing to pay all of his costs, so he didn't have a financial need to rent it. In fact, he was willing to pay someone to house-sit.

He asked Andy and Bea if they would be willing to live in his house for five years, with all expenses paid and a salary of $200 a month. They jumped at the chance and solved their housing problems in a single stroke.

CAR PURCHASES

The second most common source of debt is the purchase of a new car. Quite often a couple who can't qualify to buy a home spring for a new car as a compromise. Unfortunately, it's not a good compromise because cars now sell for prices that houses sold for twenty years ago. This is the major debt trap for most singles who overspend.

Most young people are so prone to debt-buying today that they don't even ask the price of a car—just how much the monthly payments are. I believe the automotive industry understands this mentality very well. When they want to stimulate sales for a product that has been inflated out of proportion to most other consumer products, they advertise low interest rates as the biggest selling feature. Usually that is the deciding factor for a generation that has been raised on new cars and nice houses. To the young couple already in debt because of a home that is too expensive, a new car appears to be an answer to their used car problems. So they trade in the old car, which costs $75 a month to maintain, for a new car with $150 monthly payments. But it's not good economics, as they will discover in about two months (the first month is usually free).

This debt problem is actually harder to deal with than overspending on a home. In most areas, homes can be resold at or above their original purchase price because the market for used housing is still stronger than for new housing.

But a family seeking to sell an almost new car to relieve debt is usually shocked to discover how little it's worth on the open market. If it is sold at auction, which is often the case when a car is repossessed, the sale price may be half of what an identical car sells for on a lot. Typically, when a car is repossessed for failure to make the payments, the car is sold at a loss, and the lien holder sues the borrower for the difference.

The same is true of a leased car. The lease contract to pay is just as binding as a purchase agreement. If the leasing company has to repossess a leased car, it rarely will attempt to lease it again. The typical lessee wants a brand new car, not a used one. The leased car is auctioned off, and the lessee is sued for the deficiency.

I have sometimes been accused of being negative about new cars, and to some extent that is true. Over the years I have seen the bondage that buying new cars has placed on many couples. However, if someone has his finances under control and can save for the cost of a new car, it is his decision whether or not to buy one. One person may think a new car is a bad buy, while another may think it represents better value. But the one thing neither of them can disagree about is that when you borrow money to buy a new car, you are going to become surety for the loan.

For most of my adult life I never bought a new car, for two reasons: one, I didn't have the funds to pay for one; two, I couldn't see the need for one with so many good used cars available. In 1979 I was driving a ten-year-old station wagon with well over 100,000 miles on it, and I knew that I would have to buy another car within a short time. Then one of my sons attempted to back my car up our very steep driveway during a minor ice storm. Backing up our driveway in good weather was a real trick, but it was impossible in bad weather. Like most teenagers, he was not to be stymied by a "small" obstacle such as an ice storm, so he kept trying until he burned out the reverse gear.

The next time I got into my car I discovered it whirred but wouldn't move in reverse. So we got several of the neighborhood kids out and pushed the car around in the driveway so that I could pull up the hill. For several weeks I drove it anyway, while we all prayed about what kind of a car I should buy. It didn't seem logical to spend the money to repair the old wagon when it had so many miles on it.

We didn't really have enough money to buy a new car, but with my teaching schedule and frequent trips to the airport, I knew that we needed a very dependable car. During the next few weeks I discovered how many times you pull into a parking space that you have to back out of.

While we were deciding what to do, someone actually gave a car to us. But it had a lot of miles on it too, so I figured I might as well keep the one I had and give that car to a really needy family. One of my children suggested that I give away the car with no reverse, which I vetoed.

I drove my "no-reverse" car for several more months. Then, in December, someone I had counseled several years earlier dropped by to ask if we had any particular need for a car.

"Why do you ask?" I said.

"Because I am convinced that the Lord wants me to give you one," he replied as he handed me the keys to a brand-new Oldsmobile, which I drove for the next six years.

SCHEDULED DISASTERS

Do you know how to schedule a financial disaster? It is simple. Fail to plan for predictable expenses that haven't come due yet. A common example of this is failing to plan for predictable automobile maintenance. I don't know about your cars, but mine have a regular cycle of problems. About every twenty-five to thirty thousand miles they need tires, brakes, belts, spark plugs, and so on. Once I recognize that, the smart thing to do is to anticipate those expenses and budget for them.

Failure to plan this way is a major reason many people end up in debt. When the expenses occur, they must be paid, so the only alternative available is often a credit card.

Why do reasonably intelligent people fail to anticipate known expenses? Because when they try to work them into their spending plan (a budget), they don't fit. So they simply ignore those expenses until a crisis arrives. To do otherwise would require adjustments in the other areas of spending, such as housing, cars, and vacations. This is the "head in the sand" syndrome.

It is common to see this problem when one counsels engaged couples about their first year's budget. When I ask if they have developed a budget, usually they respond, "Yes, we have, and everything worked out fine."

But when I review their budget with them, it reveals that they have made no provision for clothes, visits to the doctor, car repairs, or vacations. I *might* be convinced that they have a car that doesn't break down, and bodies that don't get sick, or even teeth that don't get cavities, but I absolutely refuse to believe they won't go to Disney World the first year they're married. And since they aren't nudists, I assume they will need to replace their clothes eventually.

I recall a couple who thought they had figured out a way to beat the system. They had financial problems that resulted from all of the above symptoms. In other words, they had a home that was too expensive, two new cars, school loans, and a variety of consumer debt items from department stores. There was absolutely no way their income could ever stretch far enough to manage their expenses, so they charged nearly everything each month except their utilities (the utility company wouldn't accept credit cards). They had been able to do that for nearly three years without being delinquent on a single bill.

Their method was to charge on one card until the limit was reached and then pay that card off with two or three others. Being a good credit customer, they had no trouble getting their credit limit raised on the first card so they could charge more, and on they went for the better part of three years. Ultimately, the whole house of credit came tumbling down because it became too large to manage. When their credit binge ended, they owed nearly $23,000 in credit card debts. They were advised to go bankrupt and were considering doing so until they received notice that two of the credit card issuers were considering filing fraud charges against them. The potential consequences of that forced them to face reality and make a commitment to repay the loans. As far as I know, they are still paying $500 in monthly payments—eight years later.

Part Three

Overview of Credit, Debt, and Borrowing

17
Understanding Credit

Since we're discussing the subject of debt in this book, we also need to discuss credit. Credit and debt are not synonymous terms, although they are used interchangeably in our society. Credit can best be defined as the establishment of a mutual trust relationship between a lender and a borrower, which can be the loan of something other than money. For instance, if I lend my lawn mower to a neighbor in exchange for the use of his garden tiller, we have a credit relationship. I have extended credit (the use of my lawn mower), and he is indebted to me until I use his tiller. This is called a barter exchange and is commonly done in business.

Debt, as defined previously, is a condition that exists when a loan commitment is not met, or inadequate collateral is pledged to unconditionally satisfy a loan agreement. Borrowing is not the only way to get into debt. A court decree in a lawsuit, for instance, can result in debt. But for the purpose of this book, we'll limit our discussion to credit-related debt.

There are two important issues in the topic of credit: how to get it and how to lose it.

How to Establish Credit

Many young people get into trouble with credit because they are desperate to establish credit and because it is easy for them to qualify for more credit than they can manage.

The very best way to establish credit initially is to borrow against an acceptable asset. For example, if you have saved $1,000 and want to borrow the same amount, almost any bank will lend you $1,000 using the savings as collateral. Usually the lender will charge from 1 to 2 percent more for the loan than the prevailing savings rate. So in essence, it costs about 2 percent interest to establish a good credit history. For a one-year loan of $1,000, the net cost would be approximately $20.

Then, by using the bank as a credit reference, almost anyone can qualify for a major credit card, although the credit limit would normally be the minimum amount. I don't mean to imply that everyone should get a credit card, or that everyone will be able to manage one properly. But credit is relatively simple to establish if you have already acquired the discipline of saving.

It has been my experience that if someone who has never had credit wishes to acquire a credit card and tries enough places, somebody will issue him one. The difficulty with this method is that once the first company issues a card and the person uses it wisely, other companies will soon follow suit, and this person will be swamped with credit card applications. The temptation of too much credit is often overwhelming for a young person (or couple), and he or she can quickly be deeply in debt.

I would offer the following advice to anyone using credit cards for the first time or anyone who has ever gotten into trouble through the misuse of credit cards. It is good advice, and it will save you many problems.

1. *Never use a credit card to buy anything that is not in your budget for the month (which means, in turn, that you will need a budget).* It is tempting to use a credit card when you are on vacation and run out of your allocated vacation funds, when you need clothes but don't have the money to take advantage of the great sale in progress, when you need tires for the car but don't have the money saved, or when you're out of work and need food, utilities, and rent. Resist

that temptation because when you use a credit card as a buffer, you may fall into a trap that will take you a long time to dig yourself out of.

2. *Pay the entire credit card bill each month.* I have heard many people say they never misused their credit cards because they paid them completely each month. I have since discovered that using credit cards—or any credit—wisely is not just a matter of being able to pay them off on time. Credit cards are the number one tool for impulse buying in our society. And impulse buying is generally the prerequisite for indulgent buying. Simply put, consumers will buy things they don't need and pay more for them, using credit.

I often use a credit card when traveling, and I always pay it off each month. At one time I assumed that because I never paid any interest on credit card purchases, I was using my card wisely. I decided to challenge my own use of credit, so I stopped using the credit card for a month.

Almost immediately I began to notice that I was less prone to accept a motel's summary of the bill when I paid in cash. The most frequent overcharge was for calls that I had placed but never completed. Also I found that I had gotten lax about verifying restaurant bills because I had been using credit cards. I discovered once again that credit is less personal than cash in your pocket, and people tend to use it more carelessly.

If you don't pay the credit card charges every month, you will pay a usurious rate of interest. The dictionary defines *usury* as lending money at an exhorbitant rate of interest; an excessive rate. Paying that interest represents poor money management. In addition, by accumulating credit card charges you run the risk of *debt.*

3. *The first month you find yourself unable to pay the total charges, destroy the cards.* The problem is not the *use* of credit. It is the *misuse* of credit.

CREDIT TO AVOID

There are some sources of credit that are simply bad deals, even by today's standards. In the constant drive to create more ways for couples to borrow money, many lenders have stepped over the borderline of common sense, in my opinion. But it is the responsibility of the borrower to avoid the use of credit that encourages poor stewardship. Following are a few examples of credit sources to avoid.

BANK OVERDRAFTS

Most banks today offer what is called overdraft protection. Thus when a customer writes a check in excess of what he or she has in the bank, the check will be honored (paid by the bank).

Sounds like a good deal, doesn't it? After all, if you write a check beyond your balance, you don't want it to "bounce," do you? There would be penalties for the returned check and charges from the merchant as well. So why not take the overdraft protection?

I have counseled many couples who did take the overdraft protection and got deeply in debt as a result of it. The people who regularly overdraft are those who don't know their checkbook balances. Obviously there are those who are dishonest and purposely overdraft, but they are a minority and usually can't get overdraft protection anyway.

The overdraft protection is an enticement for couples to avoid balancing their checking accounts. Several people I have counseled were startled to find out that overdraft protection wasn't a benevolent act on the part of the bank. The overdrafts (and penalties) were charged to their credit account at 18 to 21 percent interest. Often those accounts accumulate interest from the date of transfer, not after the normal thirty days common to credit card accounts.

FINANCE COMPANY LOANS

I don't want to impugn the integrity of all finance companies; there are many honest and ethical companies in business. But in general, local finance companies, especially those not regulated by federal laws, use high pressure tactics in their operations and charge very high interest. For instance, in many states finance companies that limit their loans to $600 or less can charge interest rates that go as high as 40 percent per year!

Finance companies specialize in lending to those who can't qualify for loans through normal channels, such as banks, credit unions, or savings and loans. They also specialize in high pressure tactics to collect their money if necessary. If you are being pursued by one of these companies, you need to read the section on the Fair Debt Collection Act in Appendix B.

HOME EQUITY LOANS

Some people might wonder why I place home equity loans in this "Credit to Avoid"section. After all, home equity loans are one of the few loans still available in which the interest can be deducted from one's income taxes.

In general, these loans have several features that make them hazardous to an individual's long-term financial health. First, they encourage someone to borrow against the equity in his home when in truth he should be working to pay the remaining mortgage off. Second, the interest rates are usually floating—meaning that they can be adjusted as the prevailing interest rates change. That puts the borrower in a position in which it is nearly impossible to control future costs. Third, most of these loans (to date) are demand notes, meaning they can be called for total payment at any time. This places the debtor in the position of constant jeopardy with the lender. During a bad economy the lender is likely to call the note to renegotiate the terms or sell the collateral (your home).

THE IRS

If there is one source of credit you should diligently avoid, it is the IRS. Or to put it another way, don't live on money that you owe to the IRS. I have counseled many couples who attempted to do this, especially couples who were self-employed. They found that the IRS will attach every asset to collect their money and will force a sale at drastically reduced prices if necessary.

THE CONSUMER CREDIT PROTECTION ACT OF 1968

Remember, if you have borrowed money from someone, he does have a right to collect what is due; however, he doesn't have a right (legally) to harass you in the process. In the past, a creditor could do virtually anything he wanted—short of physical violence —in order to collect a debt, including late night calls, calls at work, and threats of legal action. But since Congress passed the Consumer Credit Protection Act of 1968, consumers have been given legal protection from such actions. A more detailed description of the act is provided in Appendix C, but I would like to summarize the pertinent points every borrower needs to understand.

Who is controlled by this act? All persons who regularly collect debts, such as attorneys, professional collection agencies, and office personnel. The key term here is "regularly." If someone only collects debts on an irregular basis, he is not covered. For example, you may owe a debt to your dentist, so he will call you to collect his money. But he doesn't perform that function on a routine basis, so he is not covered by the Consumer Credit Protection Act.

When can a collector contact you? At any time during a normal daily routine, for instance between 8:00 A.M. and 6:00 P.M. A creditor may not contact a debtor at inconvenient or unusual times, such as late evening or early morning hours.

Can a collector call your place of work? Not if you have notified him that your employer disapproves of that practice.

Can a collector call other people about your debt? A collector may call other people in order to find your current address, but he may not contact them more than once if you have an attorney. Notify him that he can contact only your attorney. Under no circumstances may a collector discuss your debt with another person other than your designated attorney or agent.

How can you stop a collector from harassing you? By writing a letter to the collector and stating that he may not contact you again, except in regard to specific legal action taken in your case. (Obviously this should be done only in extreme cases. If a creditor has no means of communication other than legal action, he will probably take immediate legal action.)

What if you don't believe you owe the money? If you believe you don't owe the money, you need to write the collector within thirty days after you are contacted for collection, stating that you don't owe the money. If you do that, the debt collector may not contact you again without sending written proof of the debt.

A debt collector is prohibited from:

1. Giving false information to frighten you.
2. Using an alias. He must give the company name and his name if you request it.
3. Using official-looking paper or forms that give the impression of being from a government agency.
4. Using profane or abusive language or threatening any bodily harm.

5. Advertising your debt, publishing a list of people who refuse to pay him, or otherwise embarrassing you.

6. Implying or stating that legal action is being taken when it is not.

7. Giving false information to a credit reporting agency to pressure you into paying a disputed bill.

8. Depositing a postdated check before the date on the check.

What are the penalties for a collector who violates the law? If you sue the collection agency and win, the penalties are court and attorney's fees, plus damages of up to $500,000, or 1 percent of the agency's net worth, whichever is lower.

Where should you report a violation? The State Attorney General's office or the office of the Federal Trade Commission (FTC) in Washington, D.C. (The FTC will provide information about how to pursue investigation of a violation.)

What can you do about disputed debts? Fortunately, most companies are honest merchants who are not seeking to collect more than what is legitimately owed them. From time to time a dispute will arise between a debtor and creditor over a bill. Usually that can be worked out by contacting the creditor directly and stating the discrepancy. It has been my experience that in most cases the company will adjust the bill immediately, if you have good records showing your objection to be valid. However, in cases where no settlement can be reached and you believe you have a valid argument against paying the bill, the small claims court in your district provides a means of settling the dispute amicably and inexpensively.

The cost of filing a case in small claims court in most states is about $50. Usually the amount of the disputed bill will govern whether the small claims court will hear the case. Generally most small claims are limited to $1,000 or less. You can choose to have an attorney represent you, although many disputes in small claims court are handled informally without attorneys.

DOOR-TO-DOOR SALES

The Consumer Credit Protection Act provides that any merchandise sold door-to-door may be returned within seventy-two hours for a full refund. That holds true for door-to-door sales of encyclopedias, cosmetics, magazines, and so forth. You need to have proof that the merchandise was returned properly and in the same condition as delivered. Generally that means a post office receipt and a copy of the letter stating that you desire to return the merchandise. The purchaser is responsible for the return postage.

UNSOLICITED MERCHANDISE

Items that are delivered to your home or business in your name but which you did not order may be kept without payment. The merchant must show proof of purchase in order to collect. Otherwise the unsolicited merchandise is yours to keep without cost.

DEFECTIVE MERCHANDISE

If you have made an honest attempt to get the merchant to repair or replace a defective item, you may legitimately stop payment on a check issued to pay for the item or stop further payments until the dispute is resolved (usually in small claims court). This does not apply to out-of-state purchases or most credit card purchases (other than with the merchant's card).

LOST OR STOLEN CREDIT CARDS

You should notify the credit card company immediately when you realize that your card is missing. You are not responsible for any unauthorized charges on your card once notification is given. In any case, you are never responsible for more than $50 worth of unauthorized charges on a lost or stolen credit card.

UNSOLICITED CREDIT CARDS

It is illegal for card issuers to send you a credit card unless you request it. However, they may send a replacement card for one that is about to expire, and you are bound by the same rules as you were for the original card.

ELECTRONIC FUNDS—TRANSFER ERRORS

In this modern electronic age, we are faced with a new set of potential problems. One of the most common is outside-teller and fund-transfer errors. What are your rights when your account is billed for fund transfers that you didn't make?

A copy of the receipt or withdrawal slip printed by the bank's machine is proof of your claim. For transactions without such proof the bank has forty-five working days to complete an investigation and show proof of the transaction. However, if the institution hasn't completed its investigation within ten working days, your account must be credited the disputed amount pending the outcome of their investigation. At the conclusion of the investigation, the bank must show proof of its case. If you disagree, the discrepancy is revolved in small claims court.

LOSS OR STOLEN EFT CARD

If you lose your electronic funds transfer (EFT) card, also called automated teller card, and notify the bank within two days, your liability is limited to $50 in unauthorized transfers. However, if you fail to notify them within two working days, your liability is $500, up to sixty days. Beyond sixty days your liability is virtually unlimited. Therefore, it is vital that you balance all bank statements in a timely fashion each month and notify the bank (in writing) of any discrepancies.

Electronic funds theft is not an unusual event in our generation. I have counseled several couples who had bank errors in fund transfers. I also know several who had their cards stolen and money illegally transferred from their accounts.

The most common method of this type of theft today occurs when someone leaves his card in the outside teller and another person finds it. In many big cities there are thieves who hang around outside tellers waiting to snatch a neglected EFT card. They also use sophisticated surveillance equipment to spot the "secret code" often necessary to complete a fund transfer.

For more detailed information regarding your rights in Electronic Funds Transfers you can write the Federal Reserve System in Washington, DC 20551 and request information on the Electronic Funds Transfer Act.

How to Determine the "Real" Interest Rate

In conclusion to this discussion on credit, it is vital that you understand how to determine the true interest rate someone is quoting to you. Prior to 1980 that was almost impossible for most consumers. Lenders would advertise a low interest rate, but often it was based on a method of calculation that actually yielded a higher return than indicated.

The Truth in Lending Act now requires that all interest be stated in Annualized Percentage Rate (APR). That establishes one standard for all interest charged, regardless of how it is calculated. Let me present an example. If you borrowed $100 for one year, and at the end of twelve months repaid $110, you had an APR of 10 percent. But suppose you borrowed $100 and made monthly payments of $9.17. At the end of one year you will have repaid $110, but the Annualized Percentage Rate would have been higher. Why? Because you didn't actually have use of the entire $100 for the whole year. The APR rate was closer to 12 percent.

Additionally, the Truth in Lending Act requires that all finance charges be clearly shown before you sign an installment contract. Many times service fees, discount points, and insurance fees can substantially increase the cost of a loan.

A lender who fails to reveal all the costs risks penalties and forfeiture of all accumulated interest. If you believe you have been the victim of unfair lending, you need to contact the attorney general's office of your state. A more complete discussion of the Truth in Lending Act can be found in Appendix C.

In the final analysis, the best protection you can have against the misuse of credit is to determine that you will control the use of credit and refuse to allow it to control you. As stated earlier, there is no substitute for personal discipline and self-control in the area of credit.

By now I trust that you understand that the misuse of credit —not credit itself—is the problem. Borrowing is not wrong but, if done unwisely, borrowing is hazardous.

Everyone should have a goal to be debt-free eventually. If you can't be debt-free right now, set a goal and work toward it.

18
Bill Consolidation Loans

When Allen and Gladis came into my office, they were obviously "stressed out." They were nervous about being there and embarrassed to tell me their story. Allen was an attorney with a local firm specializing in real estate syndications. Just four years out of law school, Allen appeared to be the epitome of success. He was rising fast in the law firm because of his quick mind and hard work. He and Gladis had just bought a home in *the* section of their city and were expecting their first child. Their situation looked good, when viewed from the outside.

Inside, however, it was a different matter. Allen had graduated from law school owing nearly $16,000 in school loans. The interest rate on the loans was far better than average, but the monthly payments were still $125 for ten years. Gladis had school loans also, but she owed only $7,000, with payments of $80 a month. The loan payments restricted their spending but were within Allen's income capacity.

Within the last two years, Allen's salary and bonus had increased from $25,000 to nearly $34,000, and the future prospects looked even better. They felt they could afford a better home and had decided to take the plunge and buy in the area where other, older members of the firm lived. The new home cost $140,000 and carried payments of $1,150 a month after a down payment of $20,000. They lacked the funds for the total down payment, but Allen arranged an $18,000 advance on his bonus to close on the house. When they moved, Gladis purchased custom curtains, drapes, and wall decorations with Allen's encouragement. He said (and believed) that what they were doing was in the best interest of his career. Before they were finished decorating and paying for moving costs, their bills totaled nearly $11,000.

By that time Gladis was beginning to feel a little nervous about their spending, particularly since they didn't have the money to pay for all their expenses. Allen told her not to worry because the sale of their first home would net enough to pay back the advance and the improvements to the new home. Indeed, they did have a contract on their first home that would net them nearly $29,000. Unfortunately, the contract had an "if" clause in it, which meant that the buyer was obligated only if he sold his home too. So Allen and Gladis bought a new home along with all the trappings based on the contingent sale of their old home, which was dependent upon the sale of the buyer's home (a lot of ifs!).

As you have probably guessed, the sale of the buyer's home fell through, so he backed out of the sale on Allen and Gladis's home. They were already in a new home with payments of more than $1,100 a month, with $11,000 in new bills, and they were continuing payments on their old home of $700 a month as well. To say the least, Gladis was uneasy about their situation; each month they fell further behind, and still their house didn't sell. She begged Allen to drop the price but he refused, stating that it was worth what they were asking.

Finally, after six months they had an offer on the house, though it was for $5,000 less than the original contract. By that time Allen was ready to sell because he faced a higher mountain of unpaid bills each month. They netted $18,000 after paying the delinquent bills. Virtually all of the remaining proceeds from the house went to repay the firm. In the meantime they had accumulated another $3,500 in debts from miscellaneous sources.

Allen finally realized that their monthly obligations were beyond his income. So he approached the bank that held his new mortgage and asked about consolidating all of their outstanding bills into one loan. By that point, he needed about $20,000 to consolidate everything. The banker was a client of Allen's firm and thought that he would be a good risk, but Allen lacked adequate collateral for a loan that size. After a great deal of negotiating, they found a way to make the loan by taking out a second mortgage on their home and assigning that year's bonus as additional collateral.

Since the monthly payments on a $20,000 loan for three years would have been beyond Allen's income range, the banker set the payments based on a ten-year payoff, but with a balloon note to be paid in seven years (the maximum time the bank would grant for a second mortgage). It was further agreed that at least $5,000 of each year's bonuses would be paid to the bank to reduce the note.

The first year everything went fine, or so it seemed. Allen earned a bonus of $15,000, bringing his earned income to nearly $40,000. He paid $5,000 on the note, put $5,000 in savings, and paid nearly $4,000 in taxes on the bonus. With the rest he and Gladis took a vacation to a ski resort that winter.

Allen kept the books at home so Gladis didn't really have a clear idea of how they were doing month by month; but she began to see late notices coming from the bank and several credit card companies. Finally she asked Allen to sit down and tell her exactly where they were financially. He confessed that he didn't really know. "It just seems like there is never enough money to pay everything we owe," he said. He agreed with Gladis that they needed to do something about their budget, but then he got busy on a new project and they never got around to it.

As the late notices became more frequent, Gladis began to complain to Allen that he had to get some help in handling their situation. He agreed but never took the time to search out the help he needed. Finally, one afternoon the whole situation came to a head when the banker called Allen at his office. "Allen, I need to see you right away. Can you come by my office this afternoon?" he asked.

"I'm really busy right now, Mr. Barnes," Allen replied as he looked over the contracts on his desk. He had been getting less and less productive as the pressures at home built. It seemed that Gladis was always mad about one thing or another anymore.

"Allen, I must see you right away," Gary Barnes insisted. "The loan committee has been reviewing your note with the bank and is recommending that we begin foreclosure on your home."

Allen felt a cold wave of fear come over him. "They can't do that, Mr. Barnes," Allen pleaded. "It would ruin me with the firm. We have very strict rules about maintaining a good image in the community."

"Come on over and let's discuss it, Allen. Maybe there is a way we can find a resolution."

Allen put down the phone, his hand shaking. He knew he had financial problems, but until that moment he hadn't realized how bad they were. He was three months behind on his first mortgage and four months behind on the second. He had been promising the bank that he would catch up on the payments when his mid-year bonus came. But that bonus had been just $4,000, and it had been used to cover draws from the firm for living expenses. Allen's manager had called him in to review his work for the past six months because his productivity had dropped off severely. He knew that the bank's repossessing his home might cost him his job, and he was only a year away from being made a full partner in the firm. His salary and bonuses would increase substantially then. He felt cold fear rising inside as he realized that not only might he not get a partnership, he might even be released from the firm.

Allen put down his work and checked out of the office, telling the receptionist he would be back in a hour or so. He entered the bank and asked if he could see Mr. Barnes, who was the vice president of the loan department. In a short while he was directed to the banker's office.

"Allen, sit down, won't you?" Mr. Barnes said politely. He walked over and closed the door to his office. "You have some severe financial problems, don't you?" he asked.

"Well, we do have some temporary problems, Mr. Barnes," he replied. "But I'll be able to clear them up when the next bonus comes."

"Allen, you need to face reality," Mr. Barnes said as he opened the file on his desk. "I took the liberty of checking into your recent credit history. You're behind on everything, even your utility payments."

"It seems like there's not enough money to make it every month," Allen explained. "But I'll be a partner in the firm in a few months, and my income will increase substantially then. Can't you extend the second mortgage? I would only need a few thousand dollars more to make it until then."

"No, I absolutely will not. It's not more money you need, and another consolidation loan won't help. You're simply digging yourself a deeper pit. You're living beyond your means and using loans to make up the difference. And you'll just continue to do so, no matter how much you make. I did you a disservice by giving you the first consolidation loan on your house. You're worse off now than you were then."

Allen slumped down in his chair. He wanted to argue with the banker, but he knew that he was telling the truth. They were worse off now, and there seemed to be no end to the flood of money going out.

"What can I do?" Allen asked in a subdued tone. "If you foreclose on my home, I may lose my job."

"Allen, I found that one of the credit card issuers is planning legal action to collect their money. You may well be facing a judgment and garnishment if they do."

Allen almost fainted when he heard that news. *That will definitely cost me my job*, he thought. "Can you help me, Mr. Barnes?" he pleaded.

"Yes, I think so; but not by advancing you any more money. The committee wouldn't allow it even if I wanted to. I want you to go to a financial counselor who will help you to work out a plan. I know him well, and we'll work with you in whatever action he decides you should take."

Allen called me for a meeting, and I asked him to come in the next day with Gladis. The solution to Allen and Gladis's problems was difficult, but not complicated.

The first step was to get an accurate picture of where they stood financially. We listed every debt and found that they had nearly $3,000 in additional debt since the consolidation loan. Basically they were back on the same track they had been on before the loan, but with greater expenses each month because of the second mortgage.

They were also delinquent on almost every debt, including a MasterCard bill that had not been paid in five months. Their basic household expenses, together with minimum payments on their debt, took 120 percent of their income, including the average bonus Allen received.

Even before Allen took on the consolidation loan, their average monthly expenses consumed over 95 percent of their income—without such costs as clothes and medical and dental bills. The consolidation loan allowed them to avoid the reality of a bad situation for a few more months. Allen made contact with the bank that issued the MasterCard, and they agreed to accept a minimum payment on the account for three months while we were working out a permanent resolution. We then contacted Mr. Barnes and arranged for the bank to accept a three-month moratorium (no payments) on the second mortgage, provided the first mortgage was brought up to date during the following month.

The plan was simple and direct. Both Allen and Gladis realized they were in over their heads financially and they had to reduce their expenses. There were only two areas that could be cut substantially: housing and autos. The house and one car had to be sold if they were ever to balance their budget. Both decisions were difficult for them to accept until all the figures were on the table and visible. Then the facts dictated the decisions. They could stay in their home until it was repossessed, or sell it voluntarily. They could drive one new car, or lose them both. These were tough facts but easy decisions.

They had only one asset that could be converted into immediate cash to pay the bank: a cash value insurance policy that Allen had owned for several years. It had nearly $3,000 in cash value, and they used it to bring the first mortgage to a current status.

They put the house up for sale and found a buyer almost immediately. They recovered enough from the sale to pay off the credit cards and all but $4,000 of the second mortgage. The bank willingly agreed to carry a note for that amount, which was paid off within the next year.

Allen and Gladis rented a nice apartment and worked hard to get their finances under control. They developed a realistic budget and even helped some of their friends learn how to live on budget.

Allen became a partner in the law firm and now, ten years later, is the senior partner in the real estate department. He instituted a policy that all young attorneys joining the firm must attend a class on budgeting and agree to live on a budget for the first year. His feeling was that if he could get them to live on a budget for a year, they would live on one forever. He tells his story to every new attorney and proudly points out that he and Gladis bought back the home they had to sell and now own it debt-free.

Is a Consolidation Loan Always Wrong?

One of the most common questions asked in counseling is, "Should we consolidate?" So the logical question a Christian needs to ask is, "Is it wrong to consolidate?"

The answer is no, not necessarily. But there are some inherent problems that must be dealt with before a consolidation loan is advisable.

First, unless the problems that created the need for a consolidation loan are corrected, you may well find yourself worse off in the long run. For instance, if the debt was created by overspending on a monthly basis, the consolidation loan won't solve that problem. It will only delay the inevitable. Until the problem of overspending is solved, no consolidation loans should ever be considered. Otherwise a year or so later all the little bills will be back again, and when they are combined with the consolidation loan, the situation will be worse.

I recommend that no one consider a consolidation loan until he has been living for six months on a budget that controls his overspending. Once you know you have the overspending under control, it may make sense to substitute one large loan at a reduced interest rate for several smaller ones at higher rates.

Second, with a consolidation loan, there is always the tendency to stop worrying once the supposed solution has been found. Many people actually spend more the month after consolidating than they ever did before, often taking vacations or buying a new TV or VCR. Why? Because they think the pressure is off and they can relax. That is a false security created by the temporary removal of financial pressure. You need to resist that urge to splurge.

Third, all too often when someone consolidates he borrows more than what is needed to pay the outstanding bills. Then he buys things he has wanted for several months but wasn't able to afford. The purchases may actually be needed items such as a refrigerator, a washing machine, or a car.

What's wrong with that? Nothing, as long as the individual has disciplined himself and saved the money to buy those things. But for those who already have discipline problems, it's just one more way to splurge.

In our generation there are almost limitless temptations to spend. Thousands of people actually make their living thinking of new ways to lend money and collect interest. Perhaps the most common method of consolidating in the late eighties is through home equity loans. Since the '86 Tax Reform Act made home loans virtually the only interest deductible on income taxes, more and more people have turned to home equity loans for consolidating.

I personally believe home equity loans are one of the worst ideas ever pushed on the average family. It encourages them to put their homes in jeopardy and borrow to buy things that they can easily do without, such as new cars.

SOURCES OF CONSOLIDATION LOANS

There are several places a couple can obtain a consolidation loan.

CASH VALUE INSURANCE

An often overlooked source of funds for consolidating is the cash value in an insurance policy. That money can be borrowed at far less than market rates normally. Even if you don't have a cash value policy, perhaps a parent does and would be willing to lend it to you.

PLEDGED COLLATERAL

Most banks will provide loans at 1 or 2 percent below the market rate, where in-bank deposits are used as collateral. Obviously, not many people needing consolidation loans have spare cash that can be used as collateral, but often family members do. This requires a high degree of trust on the part of the family member because the collateral is at risk if the loan is not repaid. I do not recommend this option unless the borrowers are in a financial counseling program where someone is monitoring their finances at least monthly.

A collateralized loan is certainly better than a co-signed note. With pledged collateral someone might lose the asset, but with a co-signer potentially he can lose what he doesn't have.

CREDIT UNIONS

Many people have access to credit union loans at lower-than-market rates. As long as all the previously mentioned cautions are observed, a credit union loan is one of the better sources of consolidation.

FAMILY LOANS

Unless the family member (usually a parent) is able and willing to lose the money, I discourage this option. I have seen many parents discouraged and hurt because their children failed to meet their financial obligations. Obviously if the parent is willing to absorb the loss (if necessary), there is nothing wrong with parental loans.

However, a word of caution to parents is in order here. If you continually bail your children out of their financial predicaments, you are doing them a great disservice. If you want to help, be sure you require your children to get the counsel they need first. Remember, more money is not the answer to most financial problems. More discipline is the answer.

RETIREMENT ACCOUNTS

Normally money saved in a retirement account, such as an IRA, should be left there for that purpose. However, if no other source of funds is available, you can invade the retirement account and withdraw funds. Be aware that there will be income taxes due and a 10 percent surtax. But when compared to borrowing from a loan company, this may be a better deal.

In past years it was possible for individuals to borrow funds from their own private retirement accounts. This is no longer possible, and doing so may jeopardize the deferred-tax status of a retirement account.

19
Dealing with Creditors

The way people deal with their creditors says a lot about their character. There's an old proverb that says, "The rich rules over the poor, and the borrower becomes the lender's slave." Many times I have seen people be offended by an especially aggressive creditor who wants his money. However, even though in our generation we have legally limited a lender's methods to collect his money, that does not negate the lender's authority over the borrower. Just ask anyone who has defaulted on a loan.

The principle to remember is always to run toward your creditors, not away from them. When I am counseling, the most difficult problem to overcome is attempting to negotiate with a creditor who has been ignored for a long time. Put yourself in the position of a creditor. Wouldn't you want to know that someone was willing to pay but couldn't, rather than to be left totally in the dark?

Unfortunately, many people who can't pay everything don't pay anything. That is also an error. Pay what you can each month, even if it's only a partial payment. And don't make unrealistic promises in order to get a creditor off your back. You need to approach a promise to pay with the same degree of caution that you would the signing of a contract. When you give your word, you need to keep it.

HAVE A WRITTEN PLAN

I have found consistently that creditors respond best to a specific request that is backed by a detailed plan in writing.

Most creditors have been deceived so many times by people making desperate promises that they have become calloused. Almost anyone under the threat of a court summons or wage attachment will make the appropriate promises. Consequently most creditors have developed an immunity to tearful pleas from delinquent debtors. However, most will respond to a written plan backed by guaranteed action on the part of a debtor.

That's why a professional counselor is often necessary in dealing with belligerent creditors. A counselor generally represents an objective third party who will enforce the agreements.

STEP 1: A DETAILED REPORT

You need to state in detail exactly how much you owe and what the minimum monthly requirements are. In *The Financial Planning Workbook* (Chicago: Moody, 1982), helpful forms are provided. Table 19.1 reproduces one of those forms and shows a typical list of outstanding debts.

Table 19.1
List of Debts

TO WHOM OWED	CONTACT / PHONE NO.	PAY OFF	PAYMENTS REMAINING	MONTHLY PAYMENT	DATE

It's vital to be totally honest and as accurate as possible. That's why I always work with both the husband and the wife in developing a debtors' list. One partner will often overlook something that the other will recall. The obvious difficulty is that if one spouse is hiding something from the other, he or she will avoid recording it in the creditor listing. Since financial problems are usually accompanied by other problems, it is not unusual for one spouse to try to continue the deception if he is afraid of the reaction the truth will evoke. If you are in debt, I encourage you to be honest with your spouse. There is no way one person alone can resolve a debt problem that affects two people.

If you're the offended party, try to control your reaction to any new revelation about your finances. Your response will often determine whether or not your spouse will be honest in the future.

If you are the offending party, you need to accept the risks involved with total honesty and lay all the finances out on the table (literally). Ultimately the truth will be revealed anyway, and the longer it is delayed, the worse the reaction will be.

STEP 2: A BUDGET

Once the creditor list is complete and accurate, the next step is to develop a budget that will tell you and the creditors how much you can pay them each month.

In Table 19.2 I have depicted a budget from a couple I counseled several years ago. The left side shows their budget based on their previous spending records. They had to reconstruct some of it from memory because a check written to a grocery store often contained money for other expenses. I recommend that if you also do that, change it. It's better to write a check only for the purchase amount. It's difficult to reconstruct the spending later, and it's too easy to spend the surplus for indulgences.

The amounts on the right represent the new budget submitted to the creditors. Notice that the amount allocated for debts doesn't match the previous monthly total calculated from the creditor's chart. The only thing that can be done is to ask the creditors to accept a lesser amount for a period of time. Before that request can be made, however, we need to know how long that period will be. Often that depends on whether or not there are assets that can be sold and how long it will take to sell them. Also the option of a consolidation loan must be considered if it will satisfy all the creditors.

Table 19.2
Budget Analysis

GROSS PER YEAR $24,000   GROSS PER MONTH $2,000

NET SPENDABLE INCOME PER MONTH $1,550

MONTHLY PAYMENT CATEGORY	EXISTING BUDGET	NEW MONTHLY BUDGET
1. Charitable Giving	$ 200	$ 200
2. Taxes	$ 250	$ 250
NET SPENDABLE INCOME (PER MONTH)	$1,550	$1,550
3. Housing	$ 625	$ 625
4. Food	$ 200	$ 175
5. Automobile(s)	$ 260	$ 140[a]
6. Insurance	$ 0	$ 125[b]
7. Debts	$ 180	$ 115[c]
8. Enter. & Recreation	$ 75	$ 50
9. Clothing	$ 25	$ 75
10. Savings	$ 25	$ 50[d]
11. Medical	$ 110	$ 85
12. Miscellaneous	$ 100	$ 110
TOTALS (Items 3 through 12)	$1,600	$1,550

[a]Sold second car
[b]Added life and health (major medical) insurance
[c]Paid off two loans with car proceeds
[d]Increased the emergency fund

Obviously, creditors are not going to agree to a plan providing them with no payments if there is no promise of an appreciable change in the future. But I have often seen creditors accept smaller payments for a period of time when there does appear to be a logical reason for the temporary reduction. If the reduced payments are within 75 percent of the actual payments, there is usually no difficulty in getting the creditors to accept a reduced payment plan indefinitely. Obviously that depends on the creditor; some are restricted by company policies. In those cases it is often necessary to appeal to higher management. In almost all cases they will require a third party to negotiate on behalf of the debtor.

Many companies have a working agreement with the national Consumers' Credit Counseling Agency, which is a nonprofit group of credit counseling agencies located in most major cities. They can usually negotiate reduced payment schedules as well as reduced interest fees.

WHAT HAPPENS WHEN A CREDITOR WON'T COOPERATE?

Most attempts to get out of debt sound great because you usually hear the success stories. But what happens when the creditors refuse to cooperate? The principle to remember is this: don't give up too soon. Often when the debts are delinquent, the original lender has already turned the account over to a collection agency. The collection agency is less prone to cooperate and more likely to sue. But unless the debt has actually been sold to a third party, the original lender can still control the proceedings.

Generally speaking, the local credit office of a national company has only limited ability to negotiate once a loan has been declared delinquent. So your best chance to reach an agreement is to request the name of the regional or district credit manager and try to work out a settlement with him. You must suggest a reasonable plan, and you will usually need a third party reference, such as a counselor.

However, there are times when the best efforts don't work. That is usually because the debtor has made frequent promises that were not kept or because he failed to respond to the many warnings the company sent out before pursuing legal action. The actions a creditor normally takes will fall into one of three areas.

REPOSSESSION

If you have borrowed for a specific asset such as a car, television, refrigerator, or furniture, and if the asset is security for the loan, a creditor has the right to repossess it according to the terms of your loan agreement.

With rare exception, those agreements give the creditor the right to repossess without written notice, if the account is delinquent. (Many states do require written notice.) Most people have heard stories of professional car repossessors who sneak into the debtor's yard and pirate away the car. Indeed that does happen, and if a repossession order has been rendered, it is legal in most states.

More common, however, is for a delinquent debtor to receive written notice that a creditor is taking action in court. Normally there is a legal waiting period (usually one month) during which you have the right to present your side, if there is a dispute. But if a debtor ignores the notification and does not appear in court, the judgment award is automatic and the creditor can and will repossess the assets.

I have received many an urgent phone call from a frantic homeowner whose house was about to be taken by foreclosure. Often I find out the day before the foreclosure hearing. It's usually too late then, unless the entire delinquent amount can be offered the lender. If a judgment has already been handed down, it may require the entire mortgage balance. Unfortunately, the lenders usually would have worked out a reasonable plan to avoid having to repossess the home, because of the expenses involved and the bad publicity that often accompanies such action. But once the legal process is started, it is difficult to abort.

Armed with a court order, a creditor can indeed come into a debtor's home to repossess an asset. If the collector is refused entry, he can simply bring a sheriff's deputy with him the next trip and order the debtor to comply. Failure to comply with the court order can result in arrest and additional expenses.

Most loan contracts contain clauses that allow the creditor to collect all costs associated with legal action or repossessions. You need to read any contracts you sign very carefully because the costs of such actions can be significant.

Once the merchandise is recovered, the creditor may choose to sell it and apply the proceeds against the outstanding debt. The difference between the loan balance and the sale proceeds is called a deficiency, and the creditor has the right to bill the debtor for that amount plus all costs associated with the repossession and sale.

GARNISHMENT

In states that allow it, a creditor can petition the court to attach the wages of a debtor once a legal judgment has been issued. This can be a great shock to the unsuspecting debtor, as well as a source of great embarrassment. Unfortunately, it usually occurs at a time when everything else is going downhill financially. I remember the first time I encountered a garnishment. A friend asked me to meet with a young couple who were having severe financial difficulties. They had misused credit cards, department store loans, retail appliance loans, and so on. They were unable to meet all their obligations and, rather than face the creditors, they had taken the traditional ostrich approach. One of the creditors was a leasing company that specialized in rent-to-own contracts for furniture and appliances. Once their account was sixty days past due, the leasing company moved swiftly and received a judgment to repossess the furniture. They then resold the furniture for a ridiculously low price to the same company that had sold it originally, and then they sued the young couple for the deficiency, plus $400 in collection fees.

The couple received notices that the company was filing suit, but they chose to ignore the warnings and did not go to court. Consequently, the company got a garnishment order and attached both of their salaries. It was a shock when the young wife's boss called her into his office and showed her the garnishment. The garnishment required that the employer withhold up to 25 percent of her wages to pay the judgment. For a family already having severe financial difficulties, that was a major crisis. The husband found that his wages were similarly attached.

Usually there is nothing that can be done once the judgment is finalized, but I remember this particular case because it had a somewhat happy ending. After some checking around, I found that the leasing company had had several complaints filed against it for re-selling repossessed furniture to the original sales outlet at prices substantially below fair market value. I also learned that the retail store had several outstanding lawsuits against it for reselling used furniture as new.

Through a local attorney, we petitioned the court and got a re-hearing. The judge withdrew the judgment and directed the leasing company to get three appraisals on the furniture in question, as well as verification that the furniture had not been previously owned by another lessee. The leasing company chose not to pursue the issue and dropped all collection proceedings against the couple. Thus the couple avoided the garnishment but needed the next four years to work out their other financial problems.

The judge later told me that he had known the leasing company was suspect and would not have issued the judgment except that the couple didn't appear for the hearing, so he had no other choice.

BAD CREDIT REPORT

In states where a creditor cannot garnishee a debtor's wages and the debt is non-collateralized (such as a credit card loan) the creditor has one last recourse: a bad credit report. Of course credi-tors will pursue collection through notices and telephone calls. But in the final analysis they must rely on the integrity of the borrower.

The purpose of a credit report is to notify other potential lenders that someone has failed to meet the conditions of a previous con-tract. The system relies on the fact that in our society people will need additional credit and thus will want to protect their credit rat-ing. The responsibility should go even further because the require-ment to repay a debt is one of personal honor and integrity.

The reporting of credit history is controlled by the Fair Credit Reporting Act. Basically this act governs the way a credit report is handled and gives the debtor certain rights.

1. *The debtor has the right to know the name and address of the agency that prepared a report used to deny credit.* To obtain that information, it is necessary to make the request in writing to any creditor that has refused credit.

2. *Anyone refused credit has the right to review his file with the reporting agency.* He also has the right to obtain a copy of the file concerning his case history. The request must be made within thirty days of notification that he has been turned down for credit.

3. *Someone who is refused credit has the right to challenge the information in the credit report if he believes that it is inaccurate.* If the dispute cannot be resolved, a letter containing the debtor's version of the dispute must be placed in the file and sent to prospective lenders.

4. *Negative information cannot be reported beyond seven years, with the exception of a bankruptcy, which can be reported for ten years.* Because the Fair Credit Reporting Act forms the foundation for all cooperative credit reporting in this country, there are several other aspects of the Act with which all consumers should be familiar. Appendix A contains a fuller description of the Fair Credit Reporting Act.

I have dealt with most of the major creditors in our country at one time or the other on the behalf of couples I have counseled and as a member of the Consumer Counseling Service Board. I have found that most creditors are willing to go to great lengths to help anyone in financial trouble who is trying to be honest and repay what is owed. But when a debtor lies and defaults on commitments that were made, he is likely to find himself faced with powerful and hostile adversaries. It is always best to be totally honest and not to make promises that cannot be kept just for the sake of temporary peace.

I also have found that few things make a better impression on a creditor than a well-thought-out budget plan, a list of all other creditors, and a credit card cut into several pieces as a testimony of your commitment.

20
Living with Bankruptcy

In 1978 there were about fifty thousand personal bankruptcies in our country, and in 1991 there were nearly eight hundred thousand personal bankruptcies in America, according to an article in the *USA Today* newspaper. Assuming the trend will continue, we can realistically expect to see three to five million bankruptcies a year by the year 2000. That statistic spells great difficulty for many smaller merchants and for the credit industry as a whole. But, even more important, it reflects a decline in the responsibility index for the average American family.

The Federal Bankruptcy Act deals with four types of bankruptcy. These bankruptcy options are identified by the chapter in which they are outlined in the Bankruptcy Act. Two deal with corporate bankruptcy, and two deal with personal bankruptcy. They are each discussed in more detail in Appendices D, E, and F of this book. Anyone considering bankruptcy action would be well advised to read the information in the appendices on bankruptcy and then contact an attorney who specializes in this area.

Chapter 11 bankruptcy. This section of the bankruptcy code details how a corporation may file for federal bankruptcy protection and continue to operate while it works out a plan to repay the creditors. Normally a corporation has three years to repay the creditors the amount that a liquidation of the assets would have provided. If it fails to do so, it faces the possibility of total dissolution under Chapter 7 of the code.

When a company files for Chapter 11 protection, the creditors have a right to petition the court to dissolve the company and distribute the available assets. If the judge agrees, the company is abolished and sold to satisfy the debts.

If the judge grants a Chapter 11 reorganization to the company, he can require the creditors to accept reduced or deferred payments and set aside all interest charges if he feels it is in the best interest of the company's survival.

This option was designed to give struggling companies, which might otherwise fail, a chance to become profitable and thus viable. For a great testimony on use of this bankruptcy law, I recommend the book *On the Waters of the World* (Chicago: Moody, 1989), which deals with the history of the Correct Craft company in Florida and its owners, Walt and Ralph Meloon.

Chapter 7 bankruptcy. If the bankruptcy judge does not think a company can realistically become viable, he can dissolve the company under Chapter 7 of the code. The company is carefully inventoried and, under the supervision of a bankruptcy trustee appointed by the court, is dissolved and the assets sold to satisfy the creditors. In most instances the creditors receive only a percentage of the original outstanding debts. Since secured debts must be satisfied before non-secured creditors are paid, often the latter receive nothing at all.

This corporate dissolution does not affect the assets or liabilities of the principals in the corporation, except to the extent of their ownership in the corporation. Debts that were personally endorsed by individuals are still collectable by the creditors, which is obviously why many creditors require the personal endorsement of a loan by the officers and board members of a corporation.

Chapter 13 bankruptcy. This action is the equivalent for individuals of a Chapter 11 bankruptcy for a corporation. It is intended to allow an individual (or a couple) to operate under court protection from their creditors for up to three years. As with the corporate bankruptcy, the couple must be able to show that a reasonable percent-age of their debts can be paid during that period.

There are very specific limits placed on the amount of debt al-lowed and on the amount of assets owned. The court usually re-quires a frequent accounting and review of the finances to ensure that the conditions are being met.

A Chapter 13 bankruptcy action can be reported by credit report-ing agencies.

Chapter 12 bankruptcy. This is a special provision for farmers under the bankruptcy code. It allows farmers a greater asset-to-debt ratio because of the requirement for land and equipment to perform their function.

Is bankruptcy always wrong?

That is not a simple question to answer. One should be respon-sible for his promises and repay what is owed. Does that mean that in the interim one should not take the legal remedy of court protec-tion until the money can be repaid? Often that is an individual deci-sion.

The issue of motive must be addressed. Is the action being tak-en to protect the legitimate rights of the creditors? I believe that an-swer can be found in asking whether or not assets are purposely being withheld from the creditors. For example, many times when someone files for corporate or personal bankruptcy protection, as-sets have been transferred to the spouse or to other family members, as in the case of Ron's partners. If a husband and wife are treated as one, then their assets must also be treated as one.

In general, the bankruptcy laws are meant to protect the debtor, not the creditor. But if the intent is merely to protect the assets of the debtor, bankruptcy is wrong. It is better to suffer the loss of all assets rather than lose one's integrity.

What about personal or corporate lawsuits?

In the present generation it is not impossible or unlikely to be sued for millions of dollars over an accident. Also, given the present climate in jury decisions, it is not uncommon to be assessed huge damage awards. Should you then file for bankruptcy protection rath-er than be wiped out financially because of an accident lawsuit?

There are no easy answers. Individual situations require individual decisions.

I personally have no difficulty with those who use the court to avoid an unreasonable judgment. But because I want to protect myself from the potential of large damage judgments, I also choose to carry a sizable liability insurance policy that covers any accident in which I am at fault. Beyond that amount I would feel the damages are punitive rather than compensatory.

Can I avoid the IRS through a bankruptcy?

Many people are under the mistaken impression that going bankrupt avoids an obligation to the IRS. Let me assure you that that is not true. The Federal Bankruptcy Code excludes several categories of debt from the set-aside provisions of the law, including federal and state income tax liabilities. Also excluded are federally backed school loans, loans from some nonprofit institutions, and secured property loans.

I have worked with many people who have undergone bankruptcy. Some chose to do so voluntarily, and others had it forced upon them by creditor actions. In both cases they quickly realized that bankruptcy is a serious matter and, at best, both sides lose. The creditors lose much of the money they are owed, and the debtors lose some of the respect they previously had. There is a stigma associated with any bankruptcy and, until the last of the creditors are repaid, it will probably remain. You can turn an otherwise negative situation into a positive one by making a commitment to repay what is legitimately owed.

21
Where to Find Help

The type of help a person in debt needs usually depends on the severity of the problems he is facing. If the problem is the overuse of credit cards and the total debt is a few hundred dollars, usually the solution can be worked out by writing up a good plan, as I described previously. In that case what is needed is a commitment to avoid further debt and a budget to verify that commitment.

If a consolidation loan is needed to help bring the monthly payments in line with the income, the help of a good volunteer counselor is beneficial. The danger of going deeper into debt is increased by the additional loan unless some monitoring takes place. That's the primary role of the volunteer counselor: to be an objective observer and provide accountability.

As the problems intensify, the need for professional help arises. If the monthly payments exceed the available income and a reduced payment plan is required, then a counselor who will intercede is almost always a necessity. Often a well-trained volunteer counselor can help negotiate lesser payments or a moratorium on some payments until assets can be sold. But if a negotiated settlement cannot be reached, then additional help is required. This may be a professional credit counselor, an accountant, or an attorney.

Once the problems have reached the legal action stage, the need for outside counsel becomes mandatory. It is critical for a debtor to understand the rules of small claims courts or perhaps the bankruptcy court. That does not mean a debtor cannot handle any of those areas without professional help; with proper knowledge anyone can do so. I have seen many counselees plead their own cases in a small claims court action and several who were able to respond to a legal judgment notice properly. But they are the exceptions. There is a proverb that says a wise man seeks the counsel of others. "Without consultation, plans are frustrated, but with many counselors they succeed." Another proverb tells us to weigh all counsel carefully, "The naive believes everything, but the prudent man considers his steps."

What can you expect from a counselor? Too often those who ask for help expect too much too soon. Consequently, they become disillusioned when the counselor doesn't have a magical formula that will make them debt-free in three months. In reality, fewer than 15 percent of the counseling cases I have seen actually needed direct financial support. With most of those, the financial help was temporary and only met basic needs.

In most cases, the answer for a couple in financial difficulties is personal discipline—not more money. There are obvious exceptions, such as families in which a major illness has occurred or elderly people who are living on fixed incomes that are lower than the poverty level. Those are needs that must be met by others and generally are not one-time needs.

If there are urgent needs such as pending foreclosures, judgments, or evictions, we obviously try to deal with those immediately. But I make clear to everyone I counsel that there are no guarantees. If a foreclosure or eviction is imminent, it may be that nothing can be done to forestall it. Usually an experienced counselor will have contacts to assist in finding temporary housing or transportation, but beyond that, his (or her) function is counseling—not funding.

From a counselor's perspective, I can't emphasize strongly enough how many people expect unrealistic results from their advisers. Unfortunately, too many counselors foster those expectations by presenting themselves as authorities on a great variety of topics, ranging from sex to finances. Those assurances do help develop strong ties to the counselor, but they are also self-defeating when the counselees discover the hard truth that there is no substitute for personal discipline.

In my more than seventeen years of counseling, I have had several counselees whom I practically adopted. They became so dependent on my input that they literally refused to make a decision without talking to me first. Most counselors have experienced that at one time or another. At first I was flattered; then I discovered that they had become so paralyzed by their own mistakes that they no longer trusted their own judgment. Sometimes that is a predictable but temporary condition. For instance, someone who has suffered a trauma such as a divorce or death of a spouse may well need the support of an adviser. But beyond a few weeks (at the very most), that can become a crippling dependency.

I say this because I'm sure that some who read this book are depending too much on a particular adviser. A counselor is there to guide you and offer alternatives but not to become a stand-in father or mother.

A good counselor will take an objective look at the total financial picture and then make recommendations that will resolve the problems permanently. The basic counseling steps are as follows:

1. *Determine the actual spending level at present.* Rarely does a couple (and never a single person) in debt know exactly how much it costs them to live each month. If they did, most would have already taken remedial action themselves. There are a variety of methods to determine how much they're presently spending. I personally begin by asking them by category how much they believe they spend each month (see Table 21.1).

Usually they have an estimated amount of spending, but rarely is it within 15 percent of the actual amount. I will add a fixed percentage for many incidental expenses such as clothing, car repairs, and vacations. Also, I know from experience that if they have never lived by a budget, their miscellaneous spending may be as much as 50 percent higher than they estimate.

2. *Have the counselees keep a record of every expenditure they have for the next month.* In rare instances, the couple has been writing checks for every purchase and their spending record can be determined from their checkbook stubs. But only rarely. As you would expect, most couples in debt resist writing down every single purchase. I

Table 21.1
Monthly Income & Expenses

INCOME PER MONTH

Salary	$1,250	
Interest	___	
Dividends	___	
Notes	___	
Rents	___	

TOTAL GROSS
INCOME   1,250

LESS:

1. Charitable Giving	125	
2. Tax	187	

NET SPENDABLE
INCOME   938

3. Housing   391

Mortgage (rent)	260
Insurance	___
Taxes	___
Electricity	52
Gas	28
Water	6
Sanitation	5
Telephone	20
Maintenance	20
Other	___

4. Food   230

5. Automobile(s)		85
Payments	___	
Gas & Oil	40	
Insurance	20	
License	3	
Taxes	4	
Maint./ Repair/ Replacement	18	

6. Insurance		39
Life	29	
Medical	10	
Other	___	

7. Debts		90
Credit Card	80	
Loans & Notes	10	
Other	___	

8. Enter. & Recreation		53
Eating Out	20	
Trips	___	
Babysitters	8	
Activities	10	
Vacation	___	
Other	15	

9.	Clothing	50	Lunches	16
10.	Savings		Subscriptions	3
11.	Medical Expenses	30	Gifts (Incl. Christmas)	10
	Doctor 10		Special Education	
	Dentist 15			
	Drugs 5		Cash	
	Other		Other	
12.	Miscellaneous	69	TOTAL EXPENSES	1,037

Toiletry, cosmetics 10

Beauty, barber 15

Laundry, cleaning 15

Allowances

INCOME VS. EXPENSE

Net Spendable Income	938
Less Expenses	1,037
	-99

try to emphasize that this procedure is only necessary for one month —not for the rest of their lives. But it does require each of them to carry a pocket notebook for the next month and write down every penny they spend.

Once there is a clear picture of the actual monthly spending, the next step is to develop a budget that will provide for all of the regular household expenses to be paid, with some money left over to pay the creditors (hopefully). As was discussed previously, this may require some adjustments in the living expenses—particularly in the areas of housing and auto.

3. *Have the counselees maintain the budget each month.* There are no quick fixes for most people who experience financial problems. As our examination of the finances of several couples showed, each had different circumstances and required unique solutions. But one common denominator was the need for accurate records and control over their spending.

In solving financial problems, accountability is a key ingredient and cannot be overemphasized. The value of consistent accountability has been proved through Alcoholics Anonymous, Weight Watchers, and other support groups. The knowledge that someone will be checking to see if the bank book is balanced and the creditors paid helps to establish discipline.

Developing a support group in the community where you live can be a great asset to others who need help and accountability as well. I know of many groups that meet as often as once a week to discuss their common problems and try to come up with practical solutions. They develop a set of financial principles and hold each other accountable to apply those principles. The effectiveness of such accountability groups cannot be overstated. The benefits of regular group interaction have been proved over and over again in family stress therapy, drug interdiction, and psychological support groups. So, if your community doesn't have a "debtor's anonymous" group, start one.

Appendix A

Your Rights Under the Fair Credit Reporting Act

If you have a charge account, a mortgage on your home, a life insurance policy, or if you have applied for a personal loan or a job, it is almost certain that somewhere there is a "file" that shows how promptly you pay your bills, whether you have been sued or arrested, if you have filed for bankruptcy, and so forth.

The companies that gather and sell such information to creditors, insurers, employers, and other businesses are called "Consumer Reporting Agencies," and the legal term for the Report is a "Consumer Report."

The Fair Credit Reporting Act became law on April 25, 1971. This act was passed by Congress to protect consumers against the circulation of inaccurate or obsolete information and to ensure that Consumer Reporting Agencies adopted fair and equitable procedures for obtaining, maintaining, and giving out information about consumers.

Under this law you can take steps to protect yourself if you have been denied credit, insurance, or employment, or if you believe you have had difficulties because of an inaccurate or an unfair Consumer Report.

SOURCE: Used by permission of the Office of Consumer Affairs, FDIC.

Your Rights Under the Fair Credit Reporting Act

You have the right:

1. To be told the name and address of the Consumer Reporting Agency responsible for preparing a Consumer Report that was used to deny you credit, insurance, or employment; or to increase the cost of credit or insurance.
2. To be told by a Consumer Reporting Agency the nature, substance, and sources (except investigative-type sources) of the information (except medical) collected about you.
3. To take anyone of your choice with you when you visit the Consumer Reporting Agency to check on your file.
4. To obtain free of charge all information to which you are entitled within thirty (30) days after receipt of a notification that you have been denied credit. Otherwise, the Consumer Reporting Agency is permitted to charge a reasonable fee for the information.
5. To be told who has received a Consumer Report on you within the preceding six months, or within the preceding two years if the report was furnished for employment purposes.
6. To have incomplete or incorrect information reinvestigated unless the Consumer Reporting Agency has reasonable grounds to believe that the dispute is frivolous or irrelevant. If the information is investigated and found to be inaccurate, or if the information cannot be verified, you have the right to have such information removed from your file.
7. To have the Consumer Reporting Agency notify those you name (at no cost to you), who have previously received the incorrect or incomplete information, that this information has been deleted from your file.
8. If a dispute between you and the Reporting Agency about information in your file cannot be resolved, to have your version of such dispute placed in the file and included in future Consumer Reports.
9. To request that the Reporting Agency send your version of the dispute to certain businesses without charge, if your request is made within thirty (30) days of the adverse action.

10. To have a Consumer Report withheld from anyone who under the law does not have a legitimate business need for the information.
11. To sue a Reporting Agency for damages if the Agency willfully or negligently violates the law and, if you are successful, to collect attorney's fees and court costs.
12. Not to have adverse information reported after seven years. One major exception is bankruptcy, which may be reported for ten years.
13. To be notified by a business that it is seeking information about you that would constitute an Investigative Consumer Report.
14. To request from the business that ordered an Investigative Consumer Report more information about the nature and scope of the investigation.
15. To discover the nature and substance (but not the sources) of the information that was collected for an Investigative Consumer Report.

What the Fair Credit Reporting Act Does Not Do

The Fair Credit Reporting Act does not:

1. Require the Consumer Reporting Agency to provide you with a copy of your file, although some agencies will voluntarily give you a copy.
2. Compel anyone to do business with an individual consumer.
3. Apply when you request commercial (as distinguished from consumer) credit or business insurance.
4. Authorize any Federal Agency to intervene on behalf of an individual consumer.
5. Require a Consumer Reporting Agency to add new accounts to your file; however, some may do so for a fee.

How to Deal with Consumer Reporting Agencies

If you want to know what information a Consumer Reporting Agency has collected about you, either arrange for a personal interview at the agency's office during normal business hours or call in advance for an interview by telephone. Some agencies will voluntarily make disclosure by mail.

The Consumer Reporting Agencies in your community can be located by consulting the "Yellow Pages" of your telephone book under such headings as "Credit" or "Credit Rating or Reporting Agencies."

The Federal Agency that supervises Consumer Reporting Agencies is the Federal Trade Commission (FTC). Questions or complaints concerning Consumer Reporting Agencies should be directed to the Federal Trade Commission, Division of Credit Practices, Washington, DC 20580.

Appendix B

The Fair Debt Collection Act

If you use credit cards, owe money on a loan, or are paying off a home mortgage, you are a "debtor." Most Americans are.

The Fair Debt Collection Practices Act was passed by Congress in 1977 to prohibit certain methods of debt collection. Of course, the law does not erase any legitimate debt you owe.

The following questions and answers may help you understand your rights under the Debt Collection Act.

What debts are covered?

Personal, family, and household debts are covered under the Act. This includes money owed for the purchase of a car, for medical care, or for charge accounts.

Adapted from materials supplied by the Federal Trade Commission.

Who is a debt collector?

A debt collector is any person (other than the creditor) who regularly collects debts owed to others. Under a 1986 amendment to the Fair Debt Collection Practices Act, this includes attorneys who collect debts on a regular basis. The Act does not apply to attorneys who only handle debt collection matters a few times a year.

How may a debt collector contact you?

A debt collector may contact you in person, by mail, telephone, or telegram. However, a debt collector may not contact you at inconvenient or unusual times or places, such as before 8:00 A.M. or after 9:00 P.M., unless you agree. A debt collector may not contact you at work if the debt collector has reason to know that your employer disapproves.

Can you stop a debt collector from contacting you?

You may stop a debt collector from contacting you by writing a letter to the collection agency telling them to stop. Once the agency receives your letter, they may not contact you again except to say there will be no further contact or to notify you that some specific action will be taken.

May a debt collector contact any other person concerning your debt?

If you have an attorney, the collector may not contact anyone but the attorney. If you do not have an attorney, a debt collector may contact other people, but only to find out where you live or work. In most cases, the collector is not allowed to tell anyone other than you or your attorney that you owe money. Collectors are usually prohibited from contacting any person more than once.

What is the debt collector required to tell you about the debt?

Within five days after you are first contacted, the debt collector must send you a written notice telling you the amount of money you owe; the name of the creditor to whom you owe the money; and what to do if you believe you do not owe the money.

What if you believe you do not owe the money?

The debt collector may not contact you if, within thirty (30) days after you are first contacted, you sent the collector a letter saying you do not owe the money. However, a debt collector can begin collection activities again if you are sent proof of the debt, such as a copy of the bill.

What types of debt collection practices are prohibited?

Harassment. Debt collectors may not harass, oppress, or abuse any person. For example, debt collectors may not:

- use threats of violence or harm to the person, property, or reputation;
- publish a list of consumers who refuse to pay their debts (except to a credit bureau);
- use obscene or profane language;
- repeatedly use the telephone to annoy someone;
- telephone people without identifying themselves;
- advertise your debt.

False statements. Debt collectors may not use any false statements when collecting a debt. For example, debt collectors may not:

- falsely imply that they are attorneys or government representatives;
- falsely imply that you have committed a crime;
- falsely represent that they operate or work for a credit bureau;
- misrepresent the amount of the debt;
- indicate that papers being sent are legal forms when they are not.

Also, debt collectors may not say that:

- you will be arrested if you do not pay your debt or that they will seize, garnishee, attach, or sell your property or wages, unless the collection agency or the creditor intends to do so and it is legal;
- actions will be taken against you that legally may not be taken.

Debt collectors may not:

- give false credit information about you to anyone;
- send you anything that looks like an official document from a court or government agency when it is not;
- use a false name.

Unfair practices. Debt collectors may not engage in unfair practices in attempting to collect a debt. For example, debt collectors may not:

- collect any amount greater than your debt, unless allowed by law;
- deposit a post-dated check before the date on the check;
- make you accept collect calls or pay for telegrams;
- take or threaten to take your property unless this can be done legally;
- contact you by postcard.

What control do you have over payment of debts?

If you owe several debts, any payment you make must be applied to the debt you choose. A debt collector may not apply a payment to any debt you believe you do not owe.

What can you do if you believe a debt collector broke the law?

You have the right to sue a debt collector in a state or federal court within one year from the date you believe the law was violated. If you win, you may recover money for the damage you suffered. Court costs and attorney's fees also can be recovered. A group of people may sue a debt collector and recover money for damages up to $500,000, or 1 percent of the collector's net worth, whichever is less.

Where can you report a debt collector?

Report any problems with a debt collector to your state attorney general's office. Many states also have their own debt collection laws, and your attorney general's office can help you determine your rights.

If you have a question about your rights under the Fair Debt Collection Practices Act, the Federal Trade Commission may be able to assist you.

Appendix C

The Consumer Credit Protection Act

The Consumer Credit Protection Act of 1968—which launched Truth in Lending—was a landmark piece of legislation. For the first time, creditors were required to state the cost of borrowing in common language so that you, the customer, could figure out exactly what the charges for borrowing would be, compare costs, and shop for credit.

THE COST OF CREDIT

THE FINANCE CHARGE AND THE ANNUAL PERCENTAGE RATE (APR)

Credit costs vary. By remembering two terms, you can compare credit prices from different sources. Under Truth in Lending, the creditor must tell you—in writing and before you sign any agreement—the finance charge and the annual percentage rate.

The finance charge. The finance charge is the total dollar amount you pay to use credit. It includes interest costs and sometimes other costs, such as service charges and some credit-related insurance premiums or appraisal fees.

For example, borrowing $100 for a year might cost you $10 in interest. If there were a service charge of $1, the finance charge would be $11.

The annual percentage rate. The annual percentage rate (APR) is the percentage cost (or relative cost) of credit on a yearly basis. This is your key to comparing cost, regardless of the amount of credit or how long you have to repay it.

All creditors—banks, stores, car dealers, credit card companies, finance companies—must state the cost of their credit in terms of the finance charge and the APR. The law says these two pieces of information must be shown to you before you sign a credit contract. Federal law does not set interest rates or other credit charges. But it does require their disclosure so that you can compare credit costs.

COST OF OPEN-END CREDIT

Open-end credit includes credit cards, department store charge cards, and check-overdraft accounts that allow you to write checks for more than your actual balance with the bank. Truth in Lending requires that open-end creditors let you know the following two terms that will affect your costs.

First, creditors must tell you the method of calculation of the finance charge. Creditors use a number of different systems to calculate the balance on which they assess finance charges. Some creditors add finance charges after subtracting payments made during the billing period. This is called the *adjusted balance* method. Other creditors give you no credit for payments made during the billing period. This is called the *previous balance* method. Under a third method—the *average daily balance* method—creditors add your balance for each day in the billing period and then divide by the number of days in the billing period.

Second, creditors must tell you when finance charges begin on your credit account, so you know how much time you have to pay your bills before a finance charge is added. Some creditors, for example, give you a thirty-day "free ride" to pay your balance in full before imposing a finance charge.

Truth in Lending does not set the rates or tell the creditor how to make interest calculations. It only requires that the creditor tell you the method that will be used. You should ask for an explanation of any terms you don't understand.

LEASING COSTS AND TERMS

Leasing gives you temporary use of property in return for periodic payments. For instance, you might consider leasing furniture for an apartment you'll use only for a year. To help you decide whether leasing is a good idea, the Truth in Leasing law requires leasing companies to give you the facts about the costs and terms of their contracts.

The law applies to personal property leased to you for more than four months for personal, family, or household use—for example, long term rentals of cars, furniture, and appliances, but not daily car rentals or leases for apartments.

Before you agree to a lease, the leasing company must give you a written statement of costs, including the amount of any security deposit, the amount of your monthly payments, and the amount you must pay for license, registration, taxes, and maintenance.

The company must also give you a written statement about terms, including any insurance you need, any guarantees, information about who is responsible for servicing the property, any standards for its wear and tear, and whether or not you have an option to buy the property.

COSTS OF SETTLEMENT ON A HOUSE

The Real Estate Settlement Procedures Act, like Truth in Lending, is a disclosure law. The Act, administered by the Department of Housing and Urban Development, requires the lender to give you, in advance, certain information about the costs you will pay when you actually get the deed to the property. This event is called settlement, and the law helps you shop for lower settlement costs.

APPLYING FOR CREDIT

The Equal Credit Opportunity Act assures that all credit applicants will be considered on the basis of their actual qualifications for credit and will not be turned away because of personal characteristics.

Different creditors may reach different conclusions based on the same set of facts. One may find you an acceptable risk, whereas another may deny you a loan.

INFORMATION THE CREDITOR CAN'T USE

The Equal Credit Opportunity Act does not guarantee that you will get credit. You must still pass the creditor's tests of credit-worthiness. But the creditor must apply these tests fairly, impartially, and without discrimination against you on any of the following grounds: age, sex, marital status, race, color, religion, national origin, or because you exercise your rights under federal credit laws.

DISCRIMINATION AGAINST WOMEN

Both men and women are protected from discrimination based on sex or marital status. But many of the law's provisions were designed to stop particular abuses that generally made it difficult for women to get credit.

The general rule is that you may not be denied credit just because you are a woman or because you are married, single, widowed, divorced, or separated.

The law also says that creditors may not require you to re-apply for credit just because you marry or become widowed or divorced. There must be some sign that your credit-worthiness has changed. For example, creditors may ask you to re-apply if you relied on your ex-husband's income to get credit initially.

IF YOU ARE TURNED DOWN

Under the Equal Credit Opportunity Act, you must be notified within thirty days after your application has been completed whether your loan has been approved or not. If credit is denied, this notice must be in writing, and it must explain the specific reasons for denying credit.

CREDIT HISTORIES FOR WOMEN

Under the Equal Credit Opportunity Act, creditors must consider the credit history of any account that women have held jointly with their husbands. Creditors must also look at the record of any account held only in the husband's name if a woman can show it also reflects her own credit-worthiness. If the record is unfavorable—for example, if an ex-husband was a bad credit risk—she can try to show that the record does not reflect her own reputation.

CORRECTING CREDIT MISTAKES

The Fair Credit Billing Act sets up a procedure for promptly correcting billing mistakes, for refusing to make credit card payments on defective goods, and for promptly crediting your payments.

Truth in Lending gives you three days to change your mind about certain mortgage contracts; it also limits your risk on lost or stolen credit cards.

BILLING ERRORS

The Fair Credit Billing Act requires creditors to correct errors promptly and without damage to your credit rating.

The law defines a billing error as any charge:

- for something you didn't buy or for a purchase made by someone unauthorized to use your account;
- that is not properly identified on your bill or is for an amount different from the actual purchase price or was entered on a date different from the purchase date;
- for something that you did not accept on delivery or that was not delivered according to agreement.

Billing errors also include:

- errors in arithmetic;
- the failure to reflect a payment or other credit to your account;
- failure to mail the statement to your current address, provided you notified the creditor of an address change at least twenty (20) days before the end of the billing period;
- a questionable item, or an item for which you need additional information.

If you think your bill is wrong, or want more information about it, follow these steps:

1. Notify the creditor in writing within sixty (60) days after the bill was mailed. Include in this letter

   - your name and account number;

- a statement of your belief that the bill contains an error and why you believe it is wrong;
- the date and suspected amount of the error or the item you want explained.

2. Pay all parts of the bill that are not in dispute. Note that while you are waiting for an answer, you do not have to pay the amount in question (the "disputed amount") or any minimum payments or finance charges that apply to it.

   The creditor must acknowledge your letter within thirty days, unless the problem can be resolved within that time. Within two billing periods—but in no case longer than ninety (90) days—either your account must be corrected or you must be told why the creditor believes the bill is correct.

   If no error is found, the creditor must send you an explanation of the reasons for that determination and promptly send a statement of what you owe.

3. If you still are not satisfied, notify the creditor in writing within the time allowed to pay your bill.

MAINTAINING YOUR CREDIT RATING

A creditor may not threaten your credit rating while you are resolving a billing dispute.

Once you have written about a possible error, a creditor is prohibited from giving out information to other creditors or credit bureaus that would damage your credit reputation. And until your complaint is answered, the creditor also may not take any action to collect the disputed amount.

After the creditor has explained the bill, you may be reported as delinquent on the amount in the dispute, and the creditor may take action to collect if you do not pay in the time allowed. Even so, you can still disagree in writing. When the matter is settled, the creditor must report the outcome to each person who has received information about the case. Remember that you may also place your own side of the story in your credit record.

Appendix D

Introduction to the Bankruptcy Act
Section 1

The term *bankruptcy* comes from two Latin words meaning "bench" and "break." Its literal meaning is "broken bench." Under Roman law, after gathering together and dividing up the assets of a delinquent debtor, the creditors would break the debtor's workbench as a punishment to the debtor and a warning to other indebted tradesmen. Bankrupts were regarded as thieves who deserved severe penalty. The Romans deprived bankrupts of their civil rights, and many other societies stigmatized them by requiring that they dress in a particular identifying garb.

Revisions to the bankruptcy laws and changes in consumer attitudes toward bankruptcy have fostered a climate in which people regard bankruptcy as a more plausible remedy for financial problems than they once did.

A revised bankruptcy code, the Bankruptcy Act of 1978, was enacted in 1978 and took effect on October 1, 1979. The code consolidated some chapters of previous law pertaining to business reorganiza-

---

Portions of this appendix are taken from *Bankruptcy: Do It Yourself*, by Janet Kosel (Nolo Press, 1987). Used by permission.

tions and sought to streamline the administration of the bankruptcy courts, but its most sweeping changes involved personal bankruptcy. This revision made bankruptcy a more attractive option to troubled debtors, especially because it increased the amount of assets that could be exempt from liquidation.

Most important, the code introduced federal asset exemptions ($7,500 of equity in a home and approximately $3,000 in other designated assets) that were considerably more generous than were most state exemptions. It also permitted each individual of a married couple to claim such exemptions, thus doubling the amount of exemptions available to married persons.

The new code also removed a provision of the old law which stated that creditors had to approve any plan for repayment. The court was given sole discretion to accept a plan offered by a petitioner. A plan was to be confirmed if the court found that it had been proposed in good faith, that the amount to be paid the creditor was not less than what would have been paid to him through liquidation, and that the debtor would be able to make the payments stipulated by the plan.

Filings for personal bankruptcy shot up in 1980 and 1981. This led to some revision of the bankruptcy code in 1984. Courts were required, for instance, to prohibit the discharge of debts that financed eve-of-bankruptcy spending sprees.

Several developments seem to have diminished the stigma once attached to bankruptcy. The simple fact that consumer credit is more widely used today has made bankruptcy less rare, and therefore has made the bankrupt individual a more common entity. In 1988 bankruptcies topped the 500,000 mark. Also, certainly the many revisions in the law and regulations concerning debtor rights—the Truth in Lending Act, the restrictions on collection tactics of creditors, the Bankruptcy Reform Act of 1978—have fostered the notion that bankruptcy is not necessarily a shameful process.

The trend toward two-earner families has added to the likelihood of bankruptcy. If people base the levels of their spending and borrowing on the total amount of their dual incomes, interruption of either income stream could jeopardize a family's financial stability.

In sum, the rise in bankruptcies since 1984 seems most readily attributable to a large rise in consumer debt, an expansion that has boosted the aggregate indebtedness of households to nearly 19 cents per dollar of disposable income. This represents nearly 300 percent more than the average family's budget can comfortably manage.

CHAPTER 11: CORPORATE REORGANIZATION

Because this book deals with personal finances and because the issues involved in corporate reorganization under Chapter 11 of the Bankruptcy Code are extremely complex, Chapter 11 is not discussed here. Those considering corporate reorganization should seek expert legal advice.

CHAPTER 7: PERSONAL FINANCIAL DISSOLUTION

OVERVIEW OF THE BANKRUPTCY PROCEDURE

In order to file for personal bankruptcy, you must first list all of your debts and all of your property. The bankruptcy court will provide sample forms.

You can stop paying on your debts the very day you take those forms, together with $90 in cash, to the bankruptcy clerk. You can also stop right away all wage attachments and deductions from your paycheck for debts to your credit union.

About a month after you file your bankruptcy papers, you must go to the courthouse for a meeting with the trustee. He or she is the person in charge of your bankruptcy. It is the trustee's job to determine if you have any property (called non-exempt property) that under the law must be turned over to your creditors. At that meeting, the trustee will ask you questions in order to determine which items (if any) of your property he or she can take.

A couple of months after that meeting, you must go to a court hearing. If you have been honest and truthful with your creditors and the trustee, the bankruptcy judge will grant you a discharge—the formal forgiveness of all debt.

In all likelihood, you won't be able to get rid of all the debts. Why? Because the law divides all debt and property into various categories—and from a debtor's point of view, some categories are more favorable than others.

WHAT ARE DEBTS?

A debt is simply the legal obligation you have to pay someone money. Debts take many different forms. Rent, mortgage payments, taxes, bills, alimony, loans, installment payments, and court judgments are a few examples. But remember, this book deals only with personal debts. If you have any business obligations, you must see a lawyer to discuss the impact of bankruptcy on them.

Debts are divided into two categories—those that are dischargeable in bankruptcy and those that are non-dischargeable in bankruptcy. A *dischargeable debt* disappears after bankruptcy. You are legally free not to repay it. Most debts are dischargeable. Typical examples include credit card purchases, rent, and medical bills.

A *non-dischargeable debt* is not affected by bankruptcy. You must still repay it. Examples of the most important non-dischargeable debts include student loans, alimony, and taxes.

Debts are also divided into two other categories: unsecured and secured. A debt is *unsecured* if you never signed a written agreement pledging some of your property to the payment of that obligation. Most unsecured debts are dischargeable, so they disappear after bankruptcy. Typical examples include most credit card and charge account purchases, and personal loans from friends and relatives.

A *secured* debt is created when you make a written promise (usually in the form of a printed security agreement) that, if you do not pay, the creditor can take some particular item of your property— either the item you purchased or perhaps another item you pledged. Examples of merchandise where secured debts are common include motor vehicles, major appliances, expensive jewelry, and furniture. Most secured debts are dischargeable in bankruptcy. But in exchange for discharging a secured debt, you must either return the secured item to the creditor or, if you want to keep the item, pay for it. Often the lender will require that a new agreement be executed after the bankruptcy discharge.

Secured debts are divided into two types. In the first type, the secured creditor sold you the property or loaned you the money to buy it. If this is the case, you must be ready to lose the secured property—unless, of course, you want to pay for it. According to law, after bankruptcy you must pay the secured creditor either the amount of the debt or the present value of the property—whichever is less—in order to keep the property you pledged.

With the second type of secured debt, the secured creditor loaned you money and you pledged property that you already owned as security. Usually you can get this debt wiped out and are free to keep the property after bankruptcy — without paying any more for it.

WHAT IS PROPERTY?

Everything you own is property, including things you can reach out and touch—a home, a car, furniture, and the like.

After bankruptcy, you are entitled to keep only what is called exempt property. The federal and state governments have prepared lists of exempt property—things they think people need to get a fresh start. If an item is on the exempt list, you can keep it. Some examples of exempt property include equity in your home or car, work tools, furniture, appliances, and clothes. Many types of exempt property are exempt only up to a certain dollar amount.

Even though an item of your property is listed as exempt, you may still lose it in bankruptcy if you pledged it as part of a secured debt that financed the purchase of the property. If the secured debt had nothing to do with the original purchase or financing of pledged household property, you do not have to pay in order to keep it.

SOME QUESTIONS AND ANSWERS

People who are thinking about bankruptcy usually have a great many questions. Here are some of the common ones.

Will I lose my job if I go through bankruptcy?

Both private employers and governmental agencies are forbidden to fire you merely because of your bankruptcy. But there are some kinds of jobs that may be jeopardized by a declaration of bankruptcy—primarily work in which the employee must be bonded, such as a jewelry clerk or a bank teller.

How long does bankruptcy take?

It usually takes only a couple of months from the day you file to the day you appear in court to be told that you have received your formal discharge from debt. But the most important date is the day you file. The court will notify your creditors so that collection efforts, repossessions, and wage garnishments will cease within a couple of days.

Will bankruptcy be listed on my credit record?

Yes. Credit agencies are allowed to keep a notation of your bankruptcy on file for ten years. They list the total amount of dischargeable debts and specify which debts have been discharged in bankruptcy. It is up to individual creditors to decide what to do with that information.

What happens to debts co-signed by friends or relatives?

Bankruptcy protects only you. If a friend or relative co-signed your loan, he or she will have to pay it, even though you do not. Legally you will not be required to reimburse your co-signing friend or relative if this happens; whether you do so is a matter between you and your conscience.

Appendix E

Chapter 13: Personal Financial Reorganization
Section 3

The whole idea of Chapter 13 is simple: to permit an individual under court supervision and protection to develop and perform a plan to pay his or her debts in whole or in part over a three-year period. Basically, Chapter 13 means learning to live within a budget.

Filing a Chapter 13 repayment plan is a lot like taking out a debt consolidation loan. You wipe out all your obligations in exchange for weekly or monthly payments to an officer of the court. Chapter 13, however, is different from any consolidation loan because

- you pay no interest or finance charges on most debts;
- you get to determine the amount of your periodic payments;
- you decide how much of your debts you are able to repay.

Chapter 13 was conceived in the early years of the Great Depression. It was first enacted law in 1937. Major revisions were made in Chapter 13 by Congress in 1978 because it had become apparent

---

Condensed from *Chapter 13: The Federal Plan to Repay Your Debts*, by Janet Kosel (Nolo Press, 1987). Used by permission.

over the years that the old law did not provide adequate relief for consumer debtors.

An Overview of Chapter 13 Proceedings

In order to actually file a Chapter 13 debt repayment plan, you must fill out the forms showing your monthly income, ordinary living expenses, and the amount left over to apply to your debts.

Filling out and filing these forms stops all creditor collection efforts. Once you have filed your papers, you can arrange to stop wage attachments as well as any automatic debt payment deductions. Under Chapter 13, all payments to creditors will be made through a court appointed trustee following the terms of your repayment plan.

About a month after you file your forms, you must go to the courthouse for a meeting with the trustee. He or she will ask you questions about your plan, your debts, and your property. The trustee will want to make sure that you were being reasonable and responsible when you designed your budget and that your plan has a good chance of success. After your meeting with the trustee, you will also have a brief meeting with a bankruptcy judge. If the judge finds that your plan complies with the law, he or she will confirm it and it will immediately go into operation.

Most plans call for repayment of all—or almost all—of your debts over a three-year period. During that time, you will pay the trustee a certain amount each month, and the trustee will take care of all your bills and deal with your creditors. If you live up to your promise and make all payments under the plan, at the end of three years you will go back to court a second time for a discharge hearing. If you have kept your promise, the judge will formally forgive any remaining balance due on all debts covered by your plan—except taxes and family support obligations.

That's the general idea, but like almost everything else, Chapter 13 repayment plans can get more complicated, especially when you start to fill in the general picture with the details. None of the rules pertaining to Chapter 13 are very difficult, though some rules are a little hard to understand at first.

SOME QUESTIONS AND ANSWERS

What's the difference between straight bankruptcy and a Chapter 13 repayment plan?

Straight bankruptcy is a legal way to make most debts disappear with no legal requirement to repay them. People whose financial problems are not as severe usually select Chapter 13; it provides a means for repaying debts over a period of time under court supervision and protection.

Can I file a Chapter 13 plan if I once filed for straight bankruptcy?

Yes. You can file for straight bankruptcy only once every six years, but you can file a Chapter 13 plan anytime—regardless of prior bankruptcy or Chapter 13 proceedings.

How much does a Chapter 13 proceeding cost?

You must pay a $60 fee when you file your repayment plan with the court. The court will also charge a small fee to administer your plan, but this charge will be deducted automatically from your regular payments.

How long do I have to repay my debts under a Chapter 13 plan?

Most repayment plans take three years.

Is there a limit on the amount of debts that can be paid under a Chapter 13 plan?

Yes. You must owe less than $100,000 in unsecured debts and $300,000 in secured debts.

Do I have to pay 100 percent of my debts under a Chapter 13 plan?

No. It works like this. Deduct your ordinary living expenses from your monthly income. Whatever is left will be paid to your creditors over the term of your repayment plan. Bear in mind, though, that if you can't pay all—or almost all—of your debts over the three-year term of your plan, Chapter 13 may not be possible.

What happens if my creditors won't agree to my repayment plan?

Filing a Chapter 13 plan is your decision alone. If you are willing to make an honest effort, and your plan is approved by the bankruptcy court, your creditors won't have any say in the matter.

Will I lose my property if I don't pay all of my debts in full under the plan?

Probably not. Filing a Chapter 13 plan is one way to keep all of your property, even though you are unable to pay all of your debts. One exception is a Purchase Money Secured Debt (an asset purchased with a loan).

What happens to debts co-signed by friends or relatives?

If a friend or relative co-signed your loan, he will have to pay whatever portion of the debt you do not pay under the Chapter 13 plan. Legally you are not required to reimburse him—it is a matter of conscience.

Should my spouse and I both file repayment plans?

If you are married, it is usually best for you and your spouse to file a Chapter 13 plan together—especially if each of you has incurred debts.

Do I have to be working in order to file a Chapter 13 repayment plan?

No—but you must have some stable and regular source of income such as wages, earnings from self-employment or investments, pensions, social security, or public benefits.

Will my employer know about my repayment plan?

He doesn't have to know. You can choose to make regular payments directly to the trustee yourself.

NOTE: Both private employers and governmental agencies are forbidden to fire you merely because you file a Chapter 13 plan. Nevertheless, there are some kinds of jobs that may be jeopardized by filing a Chapter 13 plan—primarily work in which the employee must be bonded, such as work as a jewelry clerk or bank teller. If you have any concerns about the effect of a Chapter 13 on your job, be sure to consult with your employer before you file.

What will a Chapter 13 repayment proceeding do to my credit rating?

Credit reporting agencies are allowed to keep a notation of your Chapter 13 proceedings on file for ten years. They list the total amount of your debts and specify how much you actually paid under your repayment plan.

Do I need a lawyer in order to file a Chapter 13 repayment plan?

No. Filing a Chapter 13 plan is often easier than preparing your income tax return. If you can do that, you can probably handle your repayment plan yourself.

Appendix F

The Taxpayers' Bill of Rights

FREE INFORMATION AND HELP

You have the right to information and help in complying with the tax laws. In addition to the basic instructions, the IRS makes available other information.

TAXPAYER PUBLICATIONS

The IRS publishes more than one hundred free taxpayer information publications on various subjects. One of these, Publication 910, "Guide to Free Tax Services," is a catalog of the free services the government provides. You can order these publications and any tax forms or instructions you need by calling, toll-free, 1-800-424-FORM (3676).

Adapted from Publication 1 (8-88), Department of the Treasury, Internal Revenue Service. Used by permission.

COPIES OF TAX RETURNS

If you need a copy of your tax return for an earlier year, you can get one by filling out Form 4506, "Request for Copy of Tax Form," and paying a small fee.

However, you often only need certain information, such as the amount of your reported income, the number of your exemptions, and the tax shown on the return. You can get this information free from any IRS office.

If you have trouble clearing up any tax matter with the IRS through normal channels, you can get special help from their Problem Resolution Office.

PRIVACY AND CONFIDENTIALITY

You have the right to have your personal and financial information kept confidential. You also have the right to know why the IRS is asking you for information, exactly how any information you give will be used, and what might happen if you do not give the information.

INFORMATION SHARING

Under the law, the IRS may share your tax information with state tax agencies with which they have information exchange agreements, the Department of Justice and other federal agencies under strict legal guidelines, and certain foreign governments under tax treaty provisions.

COURTESY AND CONSIDERATION

You are entitled to courteous and considerate treatment from IRS employees at all times. If you ever feel that you are not being treated with fairness, courtesy, and consideration by an IRS employee, you should tell the employee's supervisor.

PAYMENT OF ONLY THE REQUIRED TAX

You have the right to plan your business and personal finances in such a way that you will pay the least tax that is due under the law. You are liable only for the correct amount of tax. The purpose of the IRS is to apply the law consistently and fairly to all taxpayers.

FAIRNESS IF YOUR RETURN IS EXAMINED

Most taxpayers' returns are accepted as filed. But if your return is selected for examination, it does not suggest that you are dishonest. The examination may or may not result in more tax. Your case may be closed without a change. Or you may receive a refund.

ARRANGING THE EXAMINATION

Many examinations are handled entirely by mail. For information on this, get Publication 1383,"The Correspondence Process" (Income Tax Accounts), available free by calling 1-800-424-FORM (3676). If notified that your examination is to be conducted through a face-to-face interview, or you request such an interview, you have the right to ask that the examination take place at a reasonable time and place that is convenient for both you and the IRS.

REPRESENTATION

Throughout the examination, you may represent yourself, have someone else accompany you, or, with proper written authorization, have someone represent you in your absence.

RECORDINGS

You may make a sound recording of the examination if you wish, provided you let the examiner know in advance so that he or she can do the same.

REPEAT EXAMINATIONS

If your tax return was examined for the same items in either of the two previous years and resulted in no change to your tax liability, contact the IRS as soon as possible to see if they should discontinue the repeat examination.

EXPLANATION OF CHANGES

If the IRS proposes any changes to your return, they must explain the reasons for the changes. It is important that you understand the reasons for any proposed change.

INTEREST

You must pay interest on additional tax that you owe. The interest is figured from the due date of the return. But if an IRS error caused a delay in your case, and this was grossly unfair, you may be entitled to a reduction in the interest. Only delays caused by procedural or mechanical acts that do not involve the exercise of judgment or discretion qualify. If you think the IRS caused such a delay, discuss it with the examiner and file a claim.

BUSINESS TAXPAYERS

If you are in any individual business, the rights covered in this publication generally apply to you. If you are a member of a partnership or a shareholder in a small business corporation, special rules (which may be different from those described here) may apply to the examination of your partnership or corporation items. For partnerships see Publication 556, "Examination of Return, Appeal Rights, and Claims for Refund." For regular corporations see publication 542, "Tax Information on Corporations." For S corporations see Publication 589, "Tax Information on S Corporations."

An Appeal of the Examination Findings

If you do not agree with the examiner's report, you may meet with the examiner's supervisor to discuss your case further. If you still don't agree with the examiner's findings, you have the right to appeal them. IRS Publication 5, "Appeal Rights and Preparation of Protests for Unagreed Cases," explains your appeal rights in detail and describes how to appeal.

APPEALS OFFICE

You can appeal the findings of an examination within the IRS through the Appeals Office. Most differences can be settled through this appeals system. If the matter cannot be settled to your satisfaction in Appeals, you can take your case to court.

APPEALS TO THE COURTS

Depending on whether you first pay the disputed tax, you can take your case to the U.S. Tax Court, the U.S. Claims Court, or your

U.S. District Court. These courts are entirely independent of the IRS. As always, you can represent yourself or have someone admitted to practice before the court represent you.

If you have not yet paid the tax and disagree that you owe additional tax, you can take your case to the Tax Court. Ordinarily, you have ninety days from the time the IRS mails you a formal notice (called a "notice of deficiency") telling you that you owe additional tax to file a petition with the Tax Court.

If you have already paid the disputed tax in full and filed a claim for refund that was disallowed (or on which the IRS did not take action within six months), then you may take your case to the U.S. District Court or U.S. Claims Court.

RECOVERING LITIGATION EXPENSES

If the court agrees with you on most issues in your case and finds the IRS's position to be largely unjustified, you may be able to recover some of your litigation expenses. But to do this, you must have used up all the administrative remedies available to you within the IRS, including going through the Appeals system.

FAIR COLLECTION OF TAXES

If the IRS tells you that you owe tax because of a math or clerical error on your return, you have the right to ask them to send you a formal notice (a "notice of deficiency") so that you can dispute the tax, as discussed earlier. You do not have to pay the additional tax when you ask for the formal notice, if you ask within sixty days of formal notification.

If the tax is correct, you will be given a specific period of time to pay the bill in full.

PAYMENT ARRANGEMENTS

You should make every effort to pay your bill in full. However, if you can't, you should pay as much as you can and contact the IRS right away. In order to make other payment arrangements with you, the IRS may ask you for a complete financial statement to determine how you can pay the amount due. You may qualify for an installment agreement based on your financial condition, or may arrange for your employer to deduct amounts from your pay.

Only after the IRS has tried to contact you and given you the chance to pay any tax due voluntarily can they take any enforcement action (such as recording a tax lien, or levying on or seizing property). Therefore, it is very important for you to respond right away to any attempts to contact you (by mail, telephone, or personal visit).

PROPERTY THAT IS EXEMPT FROM LEVY

If the IRS seizes (levies on) your property, you have the legal right to keep

- a limited amount of personal belongings, clothing, furniture, and business or professional books and tools;
- unemployment, worker's compensation, and certain pension benefits;
- court-ordered child support payments;
- mail;
- an amount of wages, salary, and other income ($75 per week, plus $25 for each legal dependent).

If at any time during the collection process you do not agree with the collection employee, you can discuss your case with a supervisor.

ACCESS TO YOUR PRIVATE PREMISES

A court order is not generally needed for a collection employee to seize your property. However, you don't have to allow the employee access to your private premises, such as your home or the private areas of your business, if the employee does not have court authorization to be there.

WITHHELD TAXES

If the IRS believes that you were responsible for seeing that a corporation withheld taxes from its employees, and the taxes were not paid, the IRS may look to you to personally pay the unpaid taxes. If you feel that you don't owe this, you have the right to discuss the case with the collection employee's supervisor. Also, you generally have the same IRS appeal rights as other taxpayers. Because the Tax Court has no jurisdiction in this situation, you must pay at least part of the withheld taxes and file a claim for refund in order to take the matter to the U.S. District Court or U.S. Claims Court.

About the Author

Larry Burkett was born in Winter Park, Florida on March 3rd, 1939, the fifth of eight children. After completing high school in Winter Garden, Florida, he entered the U.S. Air Force where he served as an electronics technician in the Strategic Air Command.

Upon completion of his military duties, he and his wife, Judy, returned to central Florida where he worked in the space program at Cape Canaveral, Florida. While working at the space center Larry earned degrees in marketing and finance at Rollins college, Winter Park, Florida. He spent the last several years at the space center in charge of an experiments test facility that served the Mercury, Gemini, and Apollo-manned space programs.

Larry left the space center in 1970 to become vice president of an electronics manufacturing firm. In 1972 Larry put his trust and faith in Jesus Christ to guide his life—an event that had a profound effect. In 1973 he left the electronics company to join the staff of a non-profit ministry, Campus Crusade for Christ, as a financial counselor. It was during this time that he began an intense study of what the Bible says about handling money, and began to teach small groups around the country.

In 1976 Larry Burkett left the campus ministry to form a non-profit organization dedicated to teaching the biblical principles of handling money. That organization, Christian Financial Concepts, has now grown to a nationwide ministry that reaches literally millions of people.

Larry has published 16 books on finances. Sales of his books now exceed two million copies and include several national best sellers. He is heard on two daily radio broadcasts, "Money Matters" and "How to Manage Your Money," heard on nearly 1,000 outlets worldwide.

Larry and Judy Burkett have four grown children and seven grandchildren—to date. They live in Gainesville, Georgia where the headquarters of Christian Financial Concepts is now located.

Other publications by Larry include *The Coming Economic Earthquake, Your Finances in Changing Times, Financial Planning Workbook, The Illuminati, and Investing for the Future.*

Finances are an integral part of daily living and can affect us either positively or negatively. In the Bible, God gave specific guidelines to direct our lives so we can enjoy the blessings He promises us. There are more than sixteen hundred verses in the Bible that deal directly with financial situations. Only love is discussed more often than money in the New Testament, which says something about the importance of finances.

If you are interested in knowing the financial principles found in the Bible and how to apply them to your daily life, write to Christian Financial Concepts, 601 Broad Street SE, Gainesville, Georgia 30501, or call 1-800-772-1976. The biblical principles will forever change the way you think about finances and can be used as a guide for making financial decisions in accordance with God's Word.

Finances are an integral part of daily living and can affect us either positively or negatively. In the Bible, God gave specific guidelines to direct our lives so we can enjoy the blessings He promises us. There are more than sixteen hundred verses in the Bible that deal directly with financial situations. Only love is discussed more often than money in the New Testament, which says something about the importance of finances.

If you are interested in knowing the financial principles found in the Bible and how to apply them to your daily life, write to Christian Financial Concepts, 601 Broad Street SE, Gainesville, Georgia 30501, or call 1-800-722-1976. The biblical principles will forever change the way you think about finances and can be used as a guide for making financial decisions in accordance with God's Word.